BRANCHES

D0606611

WITHDRAWN
Damaged, Obsolete, or Surplus
Jackson County Library Services

J 608 BRANCHES
88 10748

DATE DUE

NOV 6 '91		
MAR 1 8 '92		
SEP 0 4 '92		
MAR 2 4 '93		
APR 0 8 '93		
OCT 2 1 '93		
OCT 2 4 '95		
OCT 1 7 1997		
FEB 2 6 1998		
MAR 1 9 '98		
SEP 1 0 '02		
MAY 28 03		
APR 01 05		

GAYLORD PRINTED IN U.S.A.

Jackson
County
Library
System

HEADQUARTERS:
413 W. Main
Medford, Oregon 97501

SMALL INVENTIONS THAT MAKE A BIG DIFFERENCE

PHOTOGRAPHS BY NATIONAL GEOGRAPHIC PHOTOGRAPHER

JOSEPH H. BAILEY

ART BY JOHN HUEHNERGARTH

BOOKS FOR WORLD EXPLORERS
NATIONAL GEOGRAPHIC SOCIETY

88 10748
JACKSON COUNTY LIBRARY SYSTEM
MEDFORD, OREGON 97501

CONTENTS

IN THE CHIPS. *A microchip does the work of hundreds of thousands of its closest ancestor, the transistor. This chip has been magnified 1,600 times. It's actually slightly smaller than the nail on your little finger. Tiny chips like this one do big jobs in all kinds of electronic equipment. You'll learn more about the chip on pages 24–25.*

Copyright © 1984 National Geographic Society
Library of Congress CIP data: P. 101

huchnergarth

THE INVENTORS

An invention often begins as one person's idea, but it doesn't always stop there. Other people make improvements, and the invention becomes more useful. The first wooden wheel thousands of years ago led eventually to the streamlined trains of today. Huge machines that weave hundreds of yards of fabric a minute developed from the handlooms of ancient times. Without a series of improvements in the art of lens making, we'd have no telescopes with which to explore the universe. A person of the Stone Age poling a crude boat would be amazed by a luxury liner—but it's only a modern extension of the simple dugout. On the next pages, you'll meet some inventors, and you'll learn how inventors come up with their ideas.

HARD WORK

First of all, what is an invention? Sometimes it's something new that turns up by accident. That happened in 1839. An American inventor named Charles Goodyear happened to drop some natural rubber mixed with sulfur onto a hot stove. The accident created vulcanized rubber. Like natural rubber, vulcanized rubber was tough and elastic. Unlike natural rubber, it did not become brittle in cold weather and sticky in hot. Goodyear's chance invention later had hundreds of uses, from rainwear to automobile tires.

More often, however, an invention results from deliberate effort. You may have heard the saying "If you build a better mousetrap, the world will beat a path to your door." Most inventors try to improve on objects or methods that are already in use. They see a need, and they set out to fill it.

All inventors have one thing in common: They are practical thinkers. They don't mind working hard to put their ideas to use—and to gather the rewards. The rewards may take the form of wealth. Or they may simply be the satisfaction of having given something useful to the world.

PATIENT INVENTOR. *In 1879, Thomas Edison (right) hit upon a way to keep electric light bulbs glowing for a long time. He had experimented for 15 months in his workshop in Menlo Park, New Jersey. He was trying to find the right material for filaments. The filament is the part that glows inside a bulb. Finally, Edison tried charred cotton thread. It glowed steadily for 40 hours. Edison went on to improve the light bulb even more. For longer lasting filaments, he tried 6,000 different plant fibers. Bamboo was the best. Manufacturers today use filaments made of a metal called tungsten.*

WE HAVE LIFT-OFF! *On the windswept beach at Kitty Hawk, North Carolina, Wilbur Wright watches as his brother, Orville, pilots their plane. The date: December 17, 1903. It was the first successful flight of a piloted, motorized airplane. Beginning years before the flight, the Wright brothers observed birds in flight and saw how they twisted their wingtips to stay balanced. The* brothers gathered all the written information about flying that they could find. As they experimented with kites and gliders, they found that most of it was wrong. All the research and experimentation finally paid off. On that windy day, the Wright brothers' biplane stayed airborne for 12 seconds—long enough to prove that people could fly in a heavier-than-air machine.*

PHONE STYLES. A single plastic cover encloses a modern telephone (left). In the 1870s, Britain's Queen Victoria used a twin sender-and-receiver set encased in ivory (below). Alexander Graham Bell invented the telephone in the mid-1870s. He also spent many years of his life designing communications devices for the deaf.

"CAN YOU HEAR ME?" In an engraving made in the late 1870s, a man shows how to operate an early telephone (above). Without the telephone, people had to meet to hold personal conversations. With the telephone, the whole world is at people's fingertips, instantly.

7

INVENTIONS AHEAD OF

Some inventions turn up at just the right moment. People take to them as eagerly as snowbound sparrows take to birdseed. Not all inventions catch on right away, however. Here are some that were ready for the public before the public was ready for them.

▲FULL STEAM AHEAD

In 1786, New Jersey inventor John Fitch thought of using steam to power a boat. Four years later, he offered the residents of Philadelphia and Trenton the first regular steamboat service. His boat used steam-powered oars. Few would ride his noisy, smoky, newfangled boat, however. Sailboats were slower—but cleaner and quieter. Stagecoach travel was more expensive—but faster. People didn't accept steamboat travel until 1807. That's when another inventor, Robert Fulton, introduced a more efficient steamboat, one with paddle wheels on the sides, on New York's Hudson River.

▲GET A HORSE!

Richard Trevithick, an Englishman, invented a steam-powered carriage in 1801. It lasted one ride. In 1803, he drove friends around London in an improved version. It raced along at 8 miles an hour (13 km/h).* Trevithick hoped that people would see his carriage—an ancestor of the automobile—as a convenient way to get about town. Few did, and no one was interested in financing it. Trevithick gave up. He turned his attention to other inventions.

◀ALL ABOARD—PLEASE!

To win a bet, Trevithick built a steam-powered locomotive in 1804—the world's first. It puffed along at 5 miles an hour (8 km/h). It could pull 5 wagons loaded with 10 tons (10 t) of iron and 70 people. The inventor won his bet—but little else. Stronger iron for tracks had to be invented to carry the heavy train safely. Trevithick tried to sell recreational rides on a smaller version of his train (left). But the noise, steam, and soot frightened people away. In 1808, Trevithick ran out of money and hope. Not until a quarter of a century later did railroad trains come into use as a practical means of transporting goods and passengers.

8

*Metric figures in this book have been rounded off.

THEIR TIME

▲TROUBLE FOR TAILORS

In Paris, France, in 1829, a poor tailor named Barthélemy Thimonnier figured out a way to make his life easier—or so he thought. He devised a machine that could stitch seams much faster than he could by hand. The sewing machine worked so well that the French army gave him a contract to make uniforms. Other tailors, however, feared that the machine might put them out of work. A mob of angry tailors broke into Thimonnier's factory. They smashed his 80 machines to pieces. Undaunted, Thimonnier kept working on his invention. By 1848, he had built an improved model, but it, too, was destroyed. It would be ten years before tailors would accept the sewing machine—and that machine would be an American model.

◀KEYED TO SUCCESS

During the 1870s, the business world was not yet ready for the typewriter. Inventor C. Latham Sholes, far left, and his daughter Lillian faced two major objections as they demonstrated Sholes's writing machine. "Too expensive and too slow," the businessmen protested. The response discouraged the inventor, but he didn't give up. At his home in Milwaukee, Wisconsin, he designed improvements for his machine. He also invented touch-typing, a system that enables a person to type fast without looking at the keys. Touch-typing was faster than handwriting. It could save both time and money. That caused businessmen's interest to perk up. By 1900, in offices all over the United States, the *clickety-clack* of typewriters was replacing the scratching of pens.

INVENTORS AT HOME...

INVENTOR JONATHAN SANTOS, *18, of Bowie, Maryland, has been designing flying gadgets for years. He made a cross-shaped boomerang (above) when he was 13. It returns to the thrower, hovers, then floats gently down.*

Inventors, you may think, are all well-trained scientists working in labs crammed with the latest technical gadgets. Not so. Many inventors have no special training or equipment—except their lively imaginations. In fact, many successful inventions have sprung from the minds of young people.

Take Jonathan Santos, of Bowie, Maryland. In 1983, Jonathan, 18, won $1,200 in prizes at the International Science and Engineering Fair, in Albuquerque, New Mexico. He had invented a fuel-saving wingtip attachment for airplanes (right). The young inventor began thinking about fuel costs when he was 14. "I wanted to take flying lessons," he says, "but they were too expensive. If I could invent something that would make flying cheaper, maybe I could afford the lessons."

Like the Wright brothers, Jonathan began studying the flight patterns of birds. He learned all he could about the flow of air over aircraft wings. Then he began designing wing attachments and testing them in a home-built wind tunnel (below). Two years and sixty designs later, he came up with an

SEEKING TO MAKE FLYING CHEAPER, *Jonathan prepares to test a wingtip attachment in a wind tunnel he built. He invented the attachment and the motion-measuring device he is holding. Jonathan will insert the device into the tunnel and through the wingtip attachment. The blower, far left, will generate winds up to 100 miles an hour (161 km/h). The measuring device will show the amount of wing lift the wind produces. It will also show the amount of drag—resistance to the wind.*

WINNING TIP. *Jonathan displays a model of his airplane wingtip attachment (right). It won a grand prize at the 1983 International Science and Engineering Fair, in Albuquerque, New Mexico. The device changes the way air flows around a wingtip as an airplane flies. Ordinarily, the swirl of air at a wingtip produces drag. Jonathan's device redirects some of that drag to produce a lifting and pushing force. The device could mean a huge saving in the fuel needed to fly a plane—up to 27 percent.*

idea he was satisfied with. His experiments showed that the device could save fuel costs by nearly one-third. Jonathan has applied for a patent.

Then there's Becky Schroeder (right), of Toledo, Ohio. When she was 10, Becky sometimes wanted to write in the dark—but how? Putting her mind to the problem, she invented the Glo-board, a glow-in-the-dark writing pad. "It's caught the interest of policemen, darkroom workers, doctors, and kids who take notes while viewing filmstrips," says Becky. She hopes someday to have a family business producing Glo-boards.

Thousands of home inventors spend spare hours—and spare cash—trying to come up with that "better mousetrap." They work in kitchen laboratories and in garage workshops. Altogether, home inventors account for 16,000 of the 70,000 U. S. patents issued annually. And what of the remaining 54,000 patents? They go to universities, to corporations, and to companies whose only business is inventing things. To learn more about these patent holders, read on.

PATENTS APLENTY. *Dominick Labino, of Grand Rapids, Ohio, holds a list of his 58 patents (left). Among his inventions are, back row, spacecraft insulating materials, left, and an industrial device, center, that records the softening point of heated glass samples. Labino also creates sculptures, middle row, from his own glass formulas. A patent certificate appears in front. Reuben Klamer (right), of Los Angeles, California, tinkers with a safety wheel he designed for roller skates. He has marketed about 200 of his inventions. One of his inspirations became the Game of Life.*

BRIGHT IDEA. Becky Schroeder, of Toledo, Ohio (above), writes a message on the Glo-board she invented when she was 10. She came up with the idea one night as she was waiting in a car for her mother to come out of a store. If only she had paper that lit up, she thought, she could spend the time doing her homework. Later, she coated a piece of cardboard with glow-in-the-dark paint and then drew lines on it. The Glo-board was created! To use the board, she lays a piece of paper over it. The glow shines through, and she's ready to write in the dark.

13

You've probably done experiments in science class that demonstrate the lessons you're learning. But have you ever done experiments aimed at coming up with something entirely new? The students on these pages have done just that.

Many inventions spring from research done at universities. These schools often have large libraries and well-equipped laboratories. They employ specialists as instructors and as researchers. Often the researchers ask students to take an active part in the projects they are working on. In many engineering schools, instructors give their students practical problems to solve. They want to teach the students to understand a problem and to

CONCRETE FRISBEES? *Yes, and they fly just as far as the plastic ones. Frank Ellert (above), a student at the University of Cincinnati, worked on an idea that really took off. He and a dozen others developed the concrete Frisbees as an engineering-class project. The idea for these Frisbees grew out of student work on concrete canoes like the one below. To build the canoe, students Jim Thomas, in front, and Tim Becker used lightweight concrete made of cement and tiny plastic beads. College projects like this one have led to some new industrial uses for concrete.*

UNIVERSITIES...

discover different ways of approaching it. As the students tackle a problem, they often invent useful objects and methods of doing things.

Every year, engineering professors at the University of Cincinnati give their students this challenge: Develop new formulas and uses for lightweight concrete. Instead of using sand or gravel, the students mix cement with lightweight materials such as tiny, hollow plastic beads. They add chemicals to make the concrete stronger and more fluid with less water. The result is lightweight and, if need be, flexible concrete. From it, the students have made some unusual items. They've made a canoe that is lighter than aluminum models. They've made Frisbees that sail as far as plastic ones. The

SPLASHING RIGHT ALONG. *An all-terrain vehicle (ATV) from the Florida Institute of Technology (above) and another from Georgia Southern College (below) churn through a creek in Fort Belvoir, Virginia. They are entries in a yearly race among students from about 50 engineering schools. In building the vehicles, student teams invent special equipment. Each team hopes its ATV will outperform the others.*

IS IT A BOAT? *Is it a car? It's both. It's an ATV (left). Students are building it at the University of Maryland. To enter the vehicle in the race, students must power it with a lawn mower engine. The students make all other decisions about the vehicle's design. Here, Mark Lewis, in front, and Bill Crider adjust supports for the driver's seat. The car frame rests on a foam-and-fiberglass surfboard. The board will keep the vehicle afloat in water.*

15

DEALING WITH WHEELS. *Leisha Peterson and Kelly Londry compare two types of bicycle wheels (above). They're deciding which to use on an HPV—a human-powered vehicle. Kelly led a team of engineering students at the University of Cincinnati who were trying to develop a fast, inexpensive pedal-powered car.*

TESTING LEG ROOM, *Richard Wozniak occupies one of four driver's seats in the HPV (below). Gary Todd, right, takes a break as Kelly bends over to make an adjustment.*

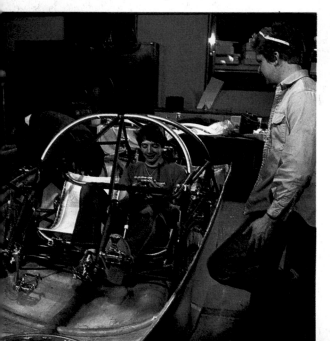

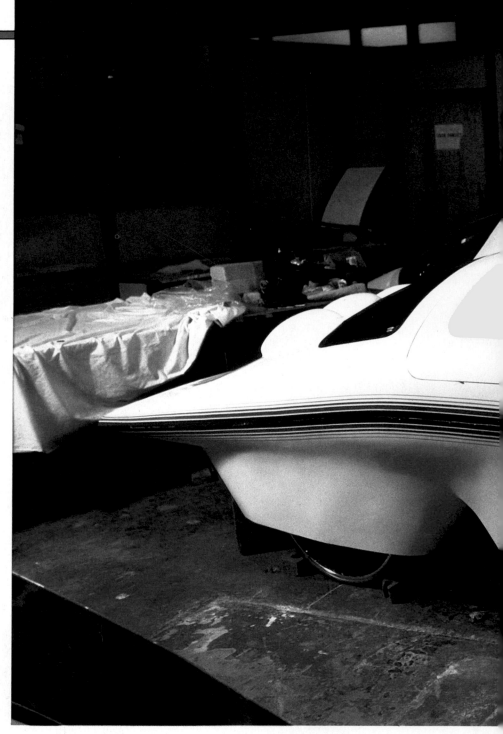

students have shown that the concrete can be used in many new ways.

At several universities, students are trying to develop new kinds of vehicles. They are designing enclosed passenger vehicles that are pedal powered. They are also developing vehicles that can move through water and over all kinds of terrain. The students may try perfecting their models in school or after graduation. If they succeed, people may someday have vehicles that are cheaper and more practical than the car or the bicycle.

Will people ever run out of things to invent? It doesn't seem likely. Every year, new products and new methods appear. As soon as they do,

people start seeking ways to improve them. Look at the electronic computer. It has been getting smaller and "smarter" ever since it first appeared in the 1940s. Such progress shows inventive minds at work.

University research has contributed greatly to such fields as computer science, medicine, engineering, and energy. Researchers working alone, as well as students challenged by instructors, have taken part. Don't get the idea, though, that inventing is all work and no play. The students on these pages would tell you that's not so. Once they finish building their experimental machines, they go out and race them—just for fun.

FINISHING TOUCHES. *Leisha and Kelly fit a door onto their HPV. The vehicle's streamlined body eliminates most drag. The body slices through the air with little resistance. On level ground, four pedalers can easily keep the car moving at about 35 miles an hour (56 km/h). "This model is only experimental," says Kelly. "But it could lead to a popular new form of transportation."*

...IN INDUSTRY...

ROBOT SAFETY. *Lee Reid's outstretched hand touches nothing, yet the yellow robot shuts off (above). All its motion stops. Reid is an engineer with the General Motors Technical Center, in Warren, Michigan. He helped invent an electronic sensing device that shuts off a robot when someone goes too near its powerful moving parts.*

Each successful invention holds the seed for many more. For example, when the motorcar became popular in the early 1900s, it created a demand for more and more driving comfort, convenience, and safety. Inventors came up with windshield wipers, headlights, seat belts, power steering, and hundreds of other things for cars. With the automobile, and with many other modern machines, the process of invention never stops.

Most inventions today result from work done in the research-and-development (R&D) laboratories of large corporations. You can think of an R&D lab as an invention factory. One of the world's largest industrial R&D labs is the General Motors Technical Center, in Warren, Michigan. In a group of 42 buildings, scientists and technicians do research and build models. They test each model, find any problems, and rework the design, if necessary. Their projects range from creating an automobile engine that runs on coal dust to designing more effective safety devices. On these and the next two pages, you'll see some exciting new ideas in the automotive world.

ELECTRONIC ROAD MAPS *will light up dashboards of the future if this invention catches on. It's a computerized navigation system, developed by a General Motors engineering team. Memory cartridges (right) hold electronically stored maps. A driver inserts a cartridge into a dashboard computer. The driver gives the computer the destination. The computer pinpoints the location of the car by interpreting special radio signals. The correct map, with a bright dot representing the car, appears on a dashboard screen. As the car moves, the dot and a lighted trail show where the car is and where it has been. The driver can call up large-area maps (above) or maps that show more detail (right). Numbers tell how many miles remain to be traveled. That makes it easy to answer one question always heard on a lengthy car trip: "How much farther is it?"*

18

LEAN INTO IT! *Jerry Williams rounds a curve in an experimental vehicle called the Lean Machine (big picture). General Motors assigned Williams and a four-man team to come up with a safe, fast, one-person vehicle that would use little fuel. The Lean Machine, designed and built over an eight-year period, meets the challenge. It can travel at 70 miles an hour (113 km/h). It covers slightly more than 100 miles (161 km) on one gallon of gasoline. The tilting of the passenger pod helps keep the vehicle from skidding or flipping in a sharp turn. Standing (small picture) or in motion, the motor pod remains upright. Williams hopes the Lean Machine will be a familiar sight someday.*

ONE A MINUTE. *That's the rate at which car frames move through this giant drilling machine (right). It does its work in an automobile manufacturing plant in Pontiac, Michigan. The Pontiac Division of General Motors, working with three private research-and-development (R&D) companies, designed and built the machine. It took years of effort. The machine helps build the Pontiac Fiero (below). Thirty-nine drills bore into a steel car frame all at one time. They drill holes in exactly the right spots. Bolts running through the holes will hold plastic body panels against the frame. The machine helps cut costs by saving time and by reducing drilling errors to nearly zero.*

DENT–RESISTANT PLASTIC, *used in the body of the Fiero, springs back into shape when twisted (below) or bumped. General Motors scientists developed the tough, flexible material as a replacement for hard-to-repair metals.*

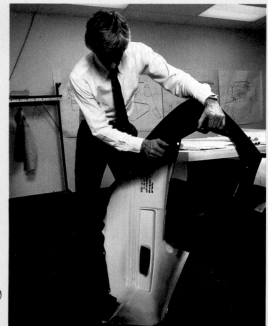

GILMAN

20

INVENTORS FOR HIRE. *Organizations and individuals often ask independent R&D groups to help turn ideas into reality. R&D firms have one specialty: invention. In the 1940s, the Battelle Memorial Institute, in Columbus, Ohio, helped an inventor improve the photocopier (above). Today, it's an essential part of most schools and offices. Read more about this invention on page 97.*

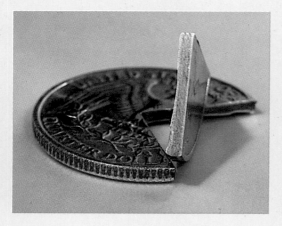

SANDWICH COIN. *In the early 1960s, the government decided to start making coins of metals that were more plentiful than silver. It turned to the Battelle Institute to find the best method. Battelle experts came up with a coin of pure copper coated with a copper-nickel mixture (above). The coating looks like silver.*

A GAS GLOWS PURPLE *as electricity flows through a vacuum chamber—an airless container. A protective plastic film will settle on the piece of foam rubber on the stand. Battelle scientists invented the plastic. They also invented the technique for applying it to various objects, using existing equipment. The process eliminates the harmful fumes of spray coating.*

S uppose, for a minute, that you are a bottle-cap manufacturer. You need to find a way to treat bottle caps so they resist acid damage. Clear plastic sprays do the job, but the fumes can harm workers. You need a better method, but you are no inventor. What do you do?

You take your problem to an independent R&D company. You pay the company to have its inventors find a solution. One large R&D group is the Battelle Memorial Institute, based in Columbus, Ohio. Battelle has solved thousands of problems since it was formed in 1929. For example, the group came up with a new plastic and a process for safely coating objects with it. The process uses electricity and a standard vacuum, or airless, chamber (below).

Battelle scientists have developed hundreds of useful things. The items range from underwater suits and tools to a quick method of making buttermilk. Business is booming. Customers of Battelle and other R&D companies number in the thousands. They include governments, businesses, and individuals from all over the world.

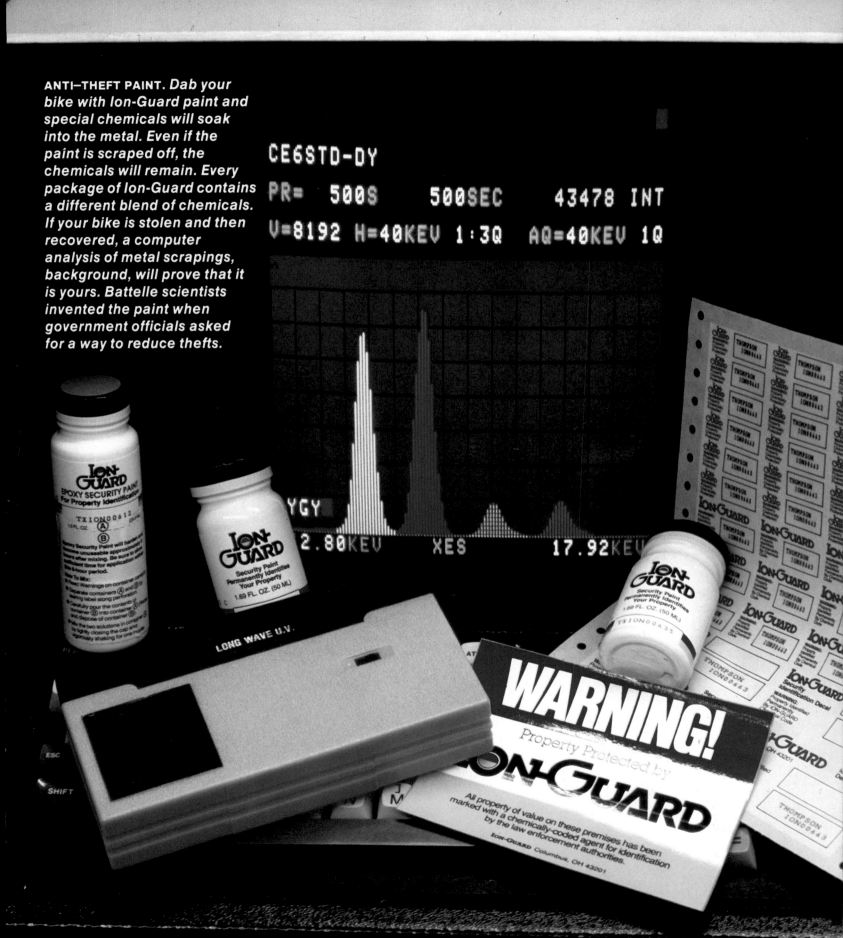

ANTI–THEFT PAINT. *Dab your bike with Ion-Guard paint and special chemicals will soak into the metal. Even if the paint is scraped off, the chemicals will remain. Every package of Ion-Guard contains a different blend of chemicals. If your bike is stolen and then recovered, a computer analysis of metal scrapings, background, will prove that it is yours. Battelle scientists invented the paint when government officials asked for a way to reduce thefts.*

THREE GENERATIONS: VACUUM TUBE TO TRANSISTOR TO MICROCHIP

1 *Listen to this! Just as the 20th century began, Lee de Forest invented the triode. This special vacuum tube could capture and amplify, or strengthen, radio signals. His small glass tube would create the science of electronics — and change the world.*

2 *In January 1915, in New York City, Alexander Graham Bell talked by telephone to his old friend Thomas Watson in San Francisco, California. Triodes along the 3,390-mile (5,456-km) circuit amplified their voices.*

Sometimes a single invention eventually results in many other new things. That's what happened when engineer Lee de Forest, in New York City, put together the triode, a three-electrode vacuum tube. An electrode is a grid or plate that sends out or collects tiny particles called electrons.

Edison had built a *two*-electrode vacuum tube, a diode. He noticed mysterious current changes in the diode, but wasn't certain what purpose they might serve. In 1904, an Englishman picked up radio waves with a diode connected to an antenna, but they were faint. De Forest in 1906 connected a *third* electrode to an antenna. His triode not only picked up radio waves that he generated in the laboratory, but it also amplified, or strengthened, them. Later, he and others made triodes that could create and transmit radio waves. Triodes opened up a whole new world: broadcasting.

Gradually, scientists found other uses for the triode. In

3 *In the 1920s, the radio became a familiar sight in many homes. Vacuum tubes made that possible. Radio stations sprang up all over the U. S. They provided news and entertainment for millions of people.*

4 *Room-size computer ENIAC, built in the mid-1940s, used 18,000 vacuum tubes. This electronic computer could complete 5,000 calculations a second. But the bulky machine used huge amounts of energy.*

9 Inside communications satellites, chips — and special-purpose transistors and vacuum tubes — help relay telephone calls around the world. Inside your phone, a single chip may handle all your dialing signals.

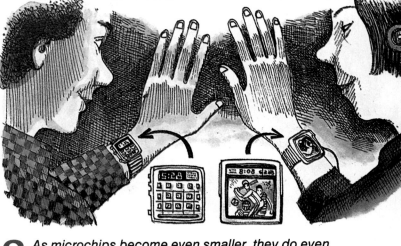

8 As microchips become even smaller, they do even more jobs. You may already wear a wrist calculator or even a wrist TV. A Japanese company began selling watch-size TVs in 1983. They may soon become as common as hand-held radios.

1945–47, they linked up thousands of the tubes as on-off switches. The result: the first electronic computer.

Vacuum tubes had drawbacks. They were bulky. They used up large amounts of energy. They gave off a lot of heat. They burned out. In 1945, three scientists at Bell Telephone Laboratories, in New York City, set out to create a better device. By 1948, they had invented the transistor. A solid crystal in a metal case, the transistor did the work of a vacuum tube without its drawbacks. It was the size of a sugar cube.

By 1959, scientists Jack Kilby, in Texas, and Robert Noyce, in California, had invented the microchip. The atoms in one chip the size of a match head now do the work once done by a roomful of tubes or by a bucketful of transistors. This grandchild of the triode shot the U. S. space program forward. It also made possible hundreds of products, from digital watches to satellites.

7 The microchip came along about 1959 and began to replace the transistor. A chip is so small and lightweight that a large ant could walk off with it. In a home computer of the 1980s, a single chip controls hundreds of thousands of electronic signals.

5 Commercial television took off in the 1940s. Early sets had relatively small screens. Big cases held a jungle of wires and vacuum tubes. The tubes received and amplified signals for both sound and picture.

6 Hand-size radios hit the beach in the 1950s. Small, energy-efficient transistors had replaced vacuum tubes. The age of miniature electronic devices had begun. Here, you see a cutaway view of a transistor. 25

GETTING A PATENT

Pick up some gadget that's around your house. Chances are you'll find a set of numbers stamped on it somewhere. Your stapler, for example, may show on the underside "Patent 2033018."

The numbers show that the inventor 1) applied to the U. S. Patent and Trademark Office, 2) learned that no one else had ever invented a stapler quite like this one, and 3) received a numbered, dated document saying so. The document—a patent—gives the inventor certain rights. It guarantees that for the next 17 years no one but the inventor can make and sell the patented item without the inventor's permission. If someone violates the patent rights, the inventor can sue in court and collect damages.

Before an invention can be patented, the patent office must make sure it hasn't been patented before. Sifting among 4½ million U. S. patents, it double-checks an earlier search by the inventor or the inventor's agent. It also checks foreign patents. If the object has been patented at any time, it cannot be patented again. The second inventor is out of luck.

FOR 92 YEARS, *the U. S. Patent Office occupied this building in Washington, D. C. Overflowing with paper, the office moved in 1932 and again in 1967. It now has large, modern quarters in Arlington, Virginia.*

HAS IT BEEN DONE? *That's what visitors to the public search room at the patent office are trying to discover. If the answer is yes, they'll know it's useless to try to obtain a patent. If the answer is no, the inventors know they have a chance. Patents protect inventors in case their ideas are copied. Shelves near this room contain 4½ million patents averaging 5 pages each.*

COMBING THE SHELVES OF THE PATENT OFFICE, *researcher Ronald Brown checks a client's idea against patents on file. Brown's clients pay him a flat fee of $185. On one search he may sift through thousands of documents. About four out of five of Brown's clients hear him report: "Sorry—somebody beat you to it." But he's saved them the high cost of applying uselessly.*

WELL, IT SEEMED

Simply obtaining a patent does not guarantee success to an inventor. If you were to examine the files of the U. S. Patent Office, you would find many thousands of inventions that never caught on—and almost certainly never will. You can see some of those inventions on these pages. The drawings are the ones actually submitted with the patent applications. You may think that these inventions range from odd to wacky. In fact, they represent various inventors' serious attempts to solve what they saw as problems. The world never beat a path to these inventors' doors, however. Perhaps people thought the solutions were worse than the problems.

(No Model.)

A. B. COWAN.
MILKING STOOL.

No. 359,921.   Patented Mar. 22, 1887.

Fig.1.

Fig.2.   *Fig.3.*

WITNESSES:
Fred G. Dietrich
John McKemon

INVENTOR:
A. B. Cowan
BY Munn & Co.
ATTORNEYS.

FEW PEOPLE GOT FIRED UP *over this 1879 invention for escaping a burning building (right). A parachute cap was supposed to slow people down as they jumped; padded shoes would break their landing. People may have thought the gear was more likely to break their necks.*

THANKS, BUT I'LL KEEP MY BIKE. *The 1885 patent for the unicycle below said the machine could be used "without any fear of danger." Even so, the vehicle rolled into the sunset, barely noticed.*

FARMER'S HELPER. *In 1887, an inventor patented this "useful improvement in milking stools" (above). It had a waist strap, a swivel seat, and a hinged back. Strapped in place, the stool would move with the milker from cow to cow. The invention never got off the ground.*

LIKE A GOOD IDEA!

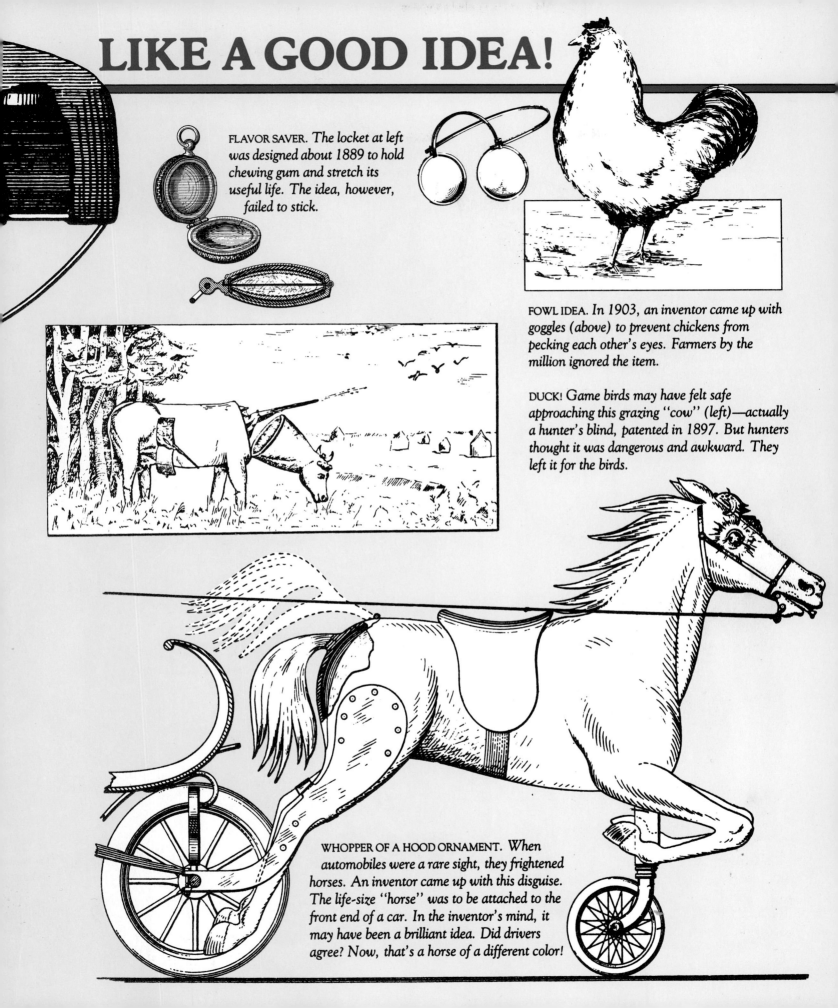

FLAVOR SAVER. *The locket at left was designed about 1889 to hold chewing gum and stretch its useful life. The idea, however, failed to stick.*

FOWL IDEA. *In 1903, an inventor came up with goggles (above) to prevent chickens from pecking each other's eyes. Farmers by the million ignored the item.*

DUCK! *Game birds may have felt safe approaching this grazing "cow" (left)—actually a hunter's blind, patented in 1897. But hunters thought it was dangerous and awkward. They left it for the birds.*

WHOPPER OF A HOOD ORNAMENT. *When automobiles were a rare sight, they frightened horses. An inventor came up with this disguise. The life-size "horse" was to be attached to the front end of a car. In the inventor's mind, it may have been a brilliant idea. Did drivers agree? Now, that's a horse of a different color!*

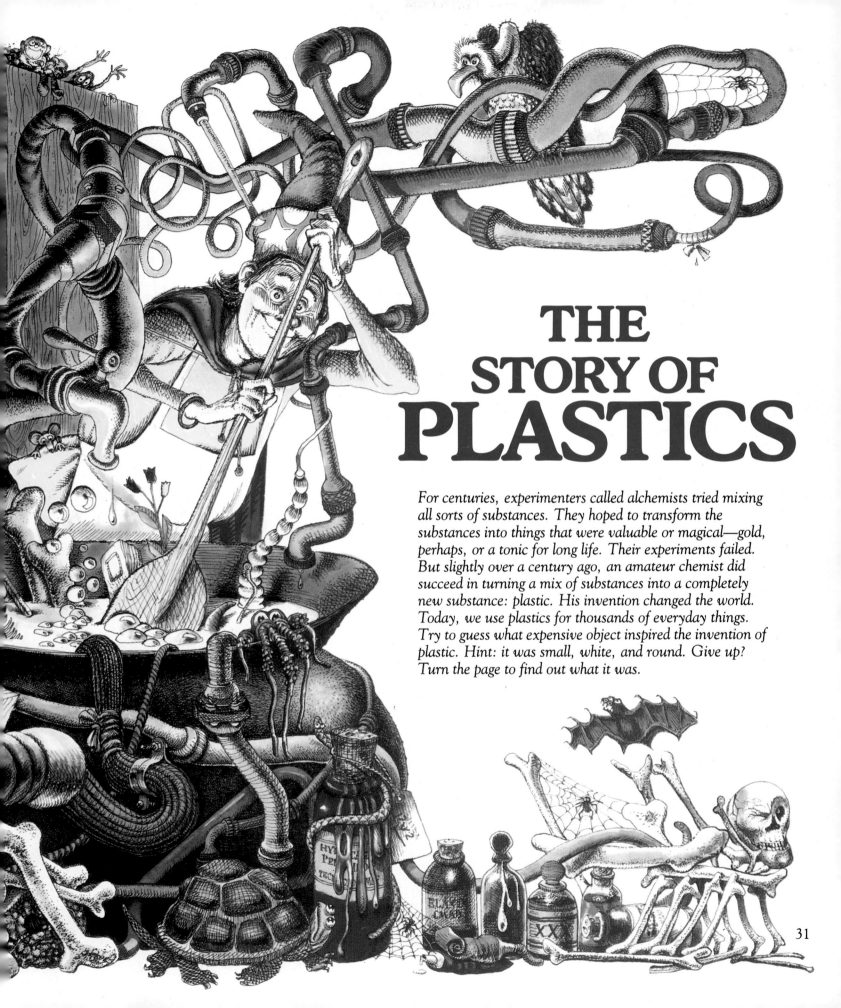

THE STORY OF PLASTICS

For centuries, experimenters called alchemists tried mixing all sorts of substances. They hoped to transform the substances into things that were valuable or magical—gold, perhaps, or a tonic for long life. Their experiments failed. But slightly over a century ago, an amateur chemist did succeed in turning a mix of substances into a completely new substance: plastic. His invention changed the world. Today, we use plastics for thousands of everyday things. Try to guess what expensive object inspired the invention of plastic. Hint: it was small, white, and round. Give up? Turn the page to find out what it was.

AN IDEA ON CUE

The search for a cheaper billiard ball—that's what led to the invention of plastics. Billiards, a gentleman's table game popular in the 1800s, used balls made of ivory. Carving them required skill and time. That made the balls expensive. In 1863, a maker of billiard balls offered a prize of $10,000 to anyone who could create a practical substitute for ivory.

John Wesley Hyatt, a printer in Albany, New York, set out to win the prize. For several years, he tried molding balls of sawdust and glue. Then he tried coating the balls with a certain liquid that dried hard and smooth. Chemists made the liquid by adding alcohol and ether to cotton treated with acids. The treated cotton is called nitrocellulose (NYE-tro-CELL-you-loce).

Hyatt experimented with this liquid, even adding ivory dust. Still, the coating was a long way from ivory. Then inspiration hit him: Why not mix the acid-treated cotton with something that left a moldable *solid* instead of a liquid? He tried powdered camphor, a substance from a tree. The camphor and a dash of alcohol did the trick. They changed the nitrocellulose into a

BEFORE PLASTICS CAME ALONG, *many products had to be made of animal parts. Cattle horn provided the material for the combs at right. Rare tortoiseshell ended up as similar products. The combs are shown with some of the tools used to fashion them. Each comb took skill and hours of labor to make. As a result, such items could cost a lot. The invention of plastics changed all that. Now factories could produce combs like these—and just about anything else— at a fraction of the former cost, time, and labor.*

USING PLASTIC BALLS, *gentlemen of the late 1800s play billiards. An inventor developed the first moldable plastic as a cheap substitute for expensive ivory billiard balls. He called the plastic celluloid. Celluloid was used in other products as well, such as the* players' collars and shirt cuffs. The celluloid balls looked like ivory, but they behaved in unpredictable ways—as you can see. Later inventors would create plastics that looked, felt, and behaved in exactly the desired ways.*

PIONEERS IN PLASTICS. In 1870, John Wesley Hyatt (above), of Albany, New York, patented his celluloid. The material had many uses, but it burned too easily. By 1909, Leo H. Baekeland (below), of Yonkers, New York, had created a fire-resistant, all-synthetic plastic called Bakelite. It pointed the way to the invention of dozens of other plastics.

CHRISTMAS SET of the 1920s (above) was made by blow molding, a Hyatt process still used today. You'll see how it works on page 44.

33

soft solid. Hyatt put the solid into a mold. He heated it while pressing it hard, then let it cool. When Hyatt opened the mold, out plunked a hard, shiny lump—the first molded plastic.

Hyatt made billiard balls from the plastic substance, which he called celluloid. The year was 1870. Did he win the $10,000 prize? It seems not. The offer had expired. Besides, the balls behaved unpredictably. Players did not like them. But the inventor made other things from celluloid. He opened up a whole new industry. It would eventually change the world.

Celluloid had one major flaw: It caught fire easily. But by 1909, a Belgian-American chemist named Leo H. Baekeland had invented a plastic—Bakelite—that did not burn easily and would not melt. Bakelite was the first plastic that contained no plant or animal material, such as cotton or glue. It was produced entirely from chemicals obtained from coal, petroleum, and natural gas.

During the next 25 years, chemists in Germany, Britain, and the United States invented several different varieties of moldable plastic. In the mid-1930s, chemist Wallace H. Carothers and a research team made a giant leap in the plastics industry. Working at E. I. du Pont de Nemours & Co. in Wilmington, Delaware, they invented nylon. It was the first all-synthetic plastic that could be spun into fibers for making cloth. Now all types of clothing, from underwear to overcoats, could be made of plastic.

The list of plastics continues to grow. On the following pages, you'll learn about modern plastics and what they can do.

PLASTICS DON'T USUALLY FLOAT FREE. *If they did, you'd have a hard time keeping your house together. What would happen to your home if all objects in it that contain plastic suddenly started floating? Here, an artist gives you an idea. You could easily spend an hour naming all the objects. Want to try?*

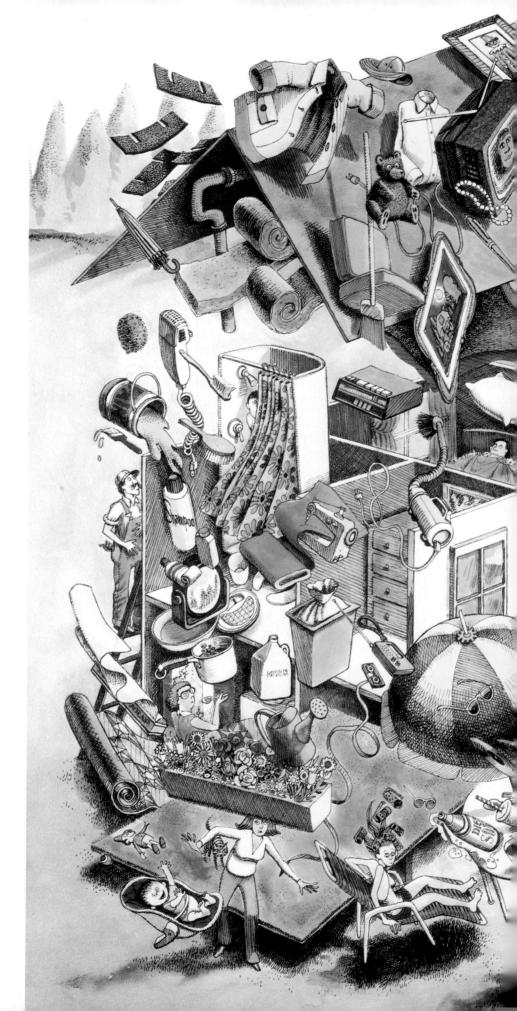

PLASTIC PRODUCTS

Manufacturers use dozens of kinds of plastic to make thousands of products. There's a plastic for nearly every job. Some plastics are hard and tough enough to stop a bullet. Others, soft as cotton balls, are made into pillows and mattresses. Manufacturers can tint plastic any color or make it as clear and colorless as crystal. They can make plastic look like wood, marble, leather, and even silver and gold. Plastics can be made as flexible as a cooked noodle or as stiff as a steel rod.

Most everyday objects you use, from automobiles to zippers, contain plastic parts. Your clothes may be woven from plastic fibers that resist staining and wrinkling. Clear plastic wrapping preserves the freshness of packaged foods. Plastic bottles let you squeeze just the right amount of mustard onto a hot dog. If you should cut your hand, a doctor may stitch up the wound with plastic thread. A plastic-base paint may brighten and protect your home. These and countless other plastic products help make everyday living safer and more comfortable.

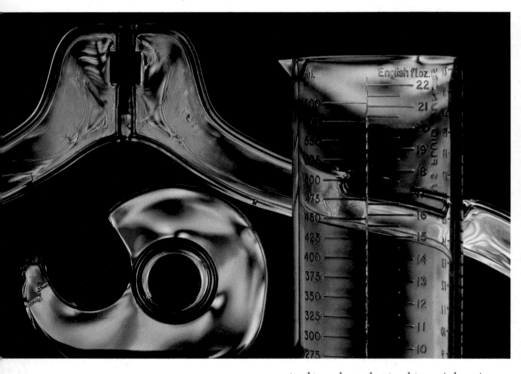

BRIGHT COLORS APPEAR *in three clear plastic objects (above) when polarized light shines through them. Manufacturers use the specially filtered light to detect weak spots. The brightest areas cooled the most quickly after molding. These areas will break more readily than the darker, slower cooling areas.*

PLASTIC PROTECTION. *A mask of plastic reinforced with fiberglass protects this ice hockey goalie's head from knocks and blows. Scratches show where swinging sticks and flying pucks have struck the mask. Tough but lightweight, the mask has been custom-molded for a perfect fit.*

STURDY PIPES. *More and more, plastic replaces metal as pipe material (below). Plastic pipes carry water and gas to buildings in many cities. Chemicals cannot corrode the pipes—that is, eat them away. Plastic pipes are lighter, cheaper, and easier to install than metal pipes.*

RED OR BLUE *or just about any other color under the sun—there's a toothbrush for every taste (below). The handles are made of a plastic called polypropylene (*PAHL-ih-PRO-puh-lean*). Trimmed fibers of nylon, another plastic, form the bristles. The bristles come in three degrees of firmness: soft, medium, and hard.*

FLYING ON PLASTIC WINGS, *pilot Bryan Allen powers and guides the Gossamer Condor on a test flight near Bakersfield, California. Plastic, cardboard, steel wire, and aluminum form the entire aircraft. The pedal-powered Condor weighs only 70 pounds (32 kg). Two years after making this flight, Allen flew a similar but even lighter craft across the English Channel. That craft, the Gossamer Albatross, was built almost entirely of plastic. It weighed 55 pounds (25 kg). Allen made the 23-mile (37-km) crossing in 2 hours, 54 minutes. For centuries, human-powered flight was just a dream. Today, it is a reality, thanks to modern engineering—and plastics.*

AUTOMOBILES OF TOMORROW *may be built almost entirely of plastics. The car below contains about 200 plastic parts. All are used in cars today, but not all are used in the same car. This car does not actually run. It simply shows the many uses of plastics in car production. The Du Pont Company assembled the parts from various American and foreign cars. Even some engine parts are plastic (left). Some modern plastics are as strong as steel, but they're lighter, cheaper, and easier to assemble. For drivers, that means lower costs and improved mileage.*

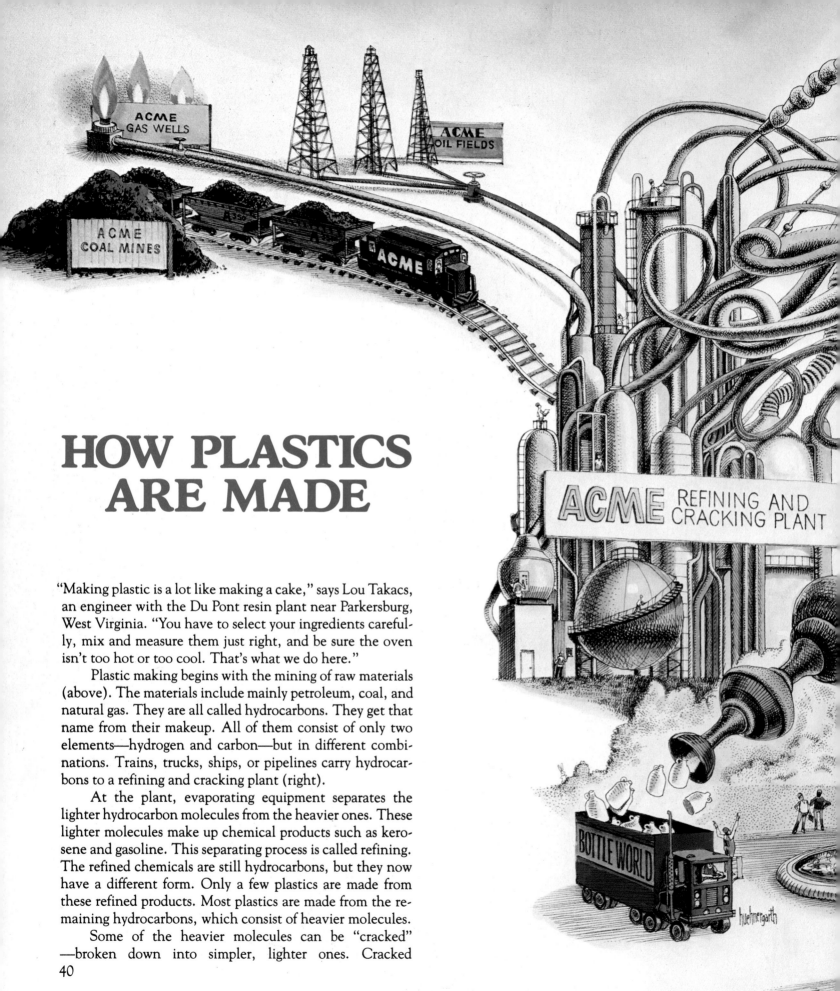

HOW PLASTICS ARE MADE

"Making plastic is a lot like making a cake," says Lou Takacs, an engineer with the Du Pont resin plant near Parkersburg, West Virginia. "You have to select your ingredients carefully, mix and measure them just right, and be sure the oven isn't too hot or too cool. That's what we do here."

Plastic making begins with the mining of raw materials (above). The materials include mainly petroleum, coal, and natural gas. They are all called hydrocarbons. They get that name from their makeup. All of them consist of only two elements—hydrogen and carbon—but in different combinations. Trains, trucks, ships, or pipelines carry hydrocarbons to a refining and cracking plant (right).

At the plant, evaporating equipment separates the lighter hydrocarbon molecules from the heavier ones. These lighter molecules make up chemical products such as kerosene and gasoline. This separating process is called refining. The refined chemicals are still hydrocarbons, but they now have a different form. Only a few plastics are made from these refined products. Most plastics are made from the remaining hydrocarbons, which consist of heavier molecules.

Some of the heavier molecules can be "cracked" —broken down into simpler, lighter ones. Cracked

40

NETWORKS OF PIPES AND TANKS *process chemicals at a Du Pont cracking plant near Orange, Texas. Cracked, or simplified, chemicals will be used to make various synthetic resins—the basic materials of plastic products. At resin-makers plants, molecules of cracked chemicals are forced together under heat and pressure. The result: resins that are totally different from the materials that produced them. Plastic starts out as petroleum, coal, or natural gas.*

molecules make up the chemicals, such as ethylene and benzene, needed to make plastics. Today, about 2 percent of all petroleum used in the U. S. ends up as plastic. The rest goes into other products.

Next, the cracked chemicals are piped to a plant where resins are made. There, more change takes place. In large mixing tanks, one or more of the chemicals are heated and pressurized. Often other chemicals, and dyes, are added. "The secret here," says Takacs, "is getting the proper formula, or recipe." The heat and pressure force the various kinds of simple molecules to link up as new, longer molecules called polymers (PAHL-uh-merz). The polymers form a new substance, the synthetic resin we call plastic.

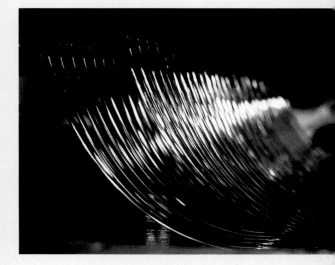

HOT, THICK LIQUID RESIN *streams from holes in a plate at the bottom of a tank (below). The liquid lands on a moving belt at the bottom of a trough of cold water. The coolness hardens the liquid into cordlike strands. Finished resin, cut into rice-size pellets, will go to manufacturing plants for molding. By altering the mix of ingredients, chemists make different resins to suit different needs.*

RESEMBLING BRIGHT BEADS, *resin pellets (below) show only a few of the colors that plastics can be tinted. Pellets like these become products ranging from toys and fabrics to medical equipment and heavy building materials.*

Resin leaves the mixing tanks as a warm, syrupy liquid. It squirts in long, spaghetti-like strands onto a moving belt in a trough of cool water. As the resin cools, it hardens. Finally, machines cut the hardened resin into rice-size pellets. The pellets (right) are shipped to factories. Manufacturers find the pellets convenient to work with. They flow easily from storage bins to molding machines. The machines melt down the pellets. Molds shape the melted resin into dishes, toys, machine parts, and thousands of other items.

"To me," says Takacs, "it's always amazing to see how we can take raw materials from the ground, mix them so that their molecules are rearranged, and turn them into plastic that is both pretty and useful."

PLASTICS SHAPE THE WORLD

INJECTION MOLDING *shapes resins into many plastic products. Here, a worker operates an injection-molding machine. The machine forces melted resin into two-piece molds. This machine is making casings for electric drills.*

Plastics have come a long way since John Wesley Hyatt first plunked that celluloid lump onto his laboratory table a little more than a century ago. Today, chemists rearrange atoms and molecules just as they wish. The plastics they make ease the demand for other resources. Imagine how much cotton, wool, metal, wood, and leather would be required today if it were not for plastic substitutes. Plastic is cheaper and often more practical than natural substances. As the world's population grows, so will the importance of plastics.

Scientists foresee climate-controlled cities under plastic domes. Space colonies, enclosed in huge plastic satellites, may someday orbit the earth. Doctors predict that very soon plastic hearts and other organ substitutes will be saving thousands of lives every year.

It's easy to forget that this huge industry really began as just one man's idea for solving a small problem: the high cost of ivory billiard balls. As with many other small but important inventions, one idea led to another, and that to another, and that—well, you get the idea.

INVENTED BY HYATT, *a process called blow molding forms hollow objects, such as plastic bottles. A limp sack made of warm, semiliquid resin appears from a hole near the top of a mold (above). The mold's two halves then clamp shut around the sack. Air is pumped in, and the sack expands like a balloon against the mold, taking its shape in every detail. This machine can make a bottle (right) every 15 seconds.*

44

GIANT BUBBLE OF PLASTIC *shoots high over a worker's head from a machine called a blow extruder. Air blows melted resin up through a ring-shaped opening. The resin flows out as an endless cylinder of plastic film. It will become a roll of garment bags. Rollers in the top right corner flatten the cylinder. Other equipment seals off bags and punches holes for tearing the bags from the roll.*

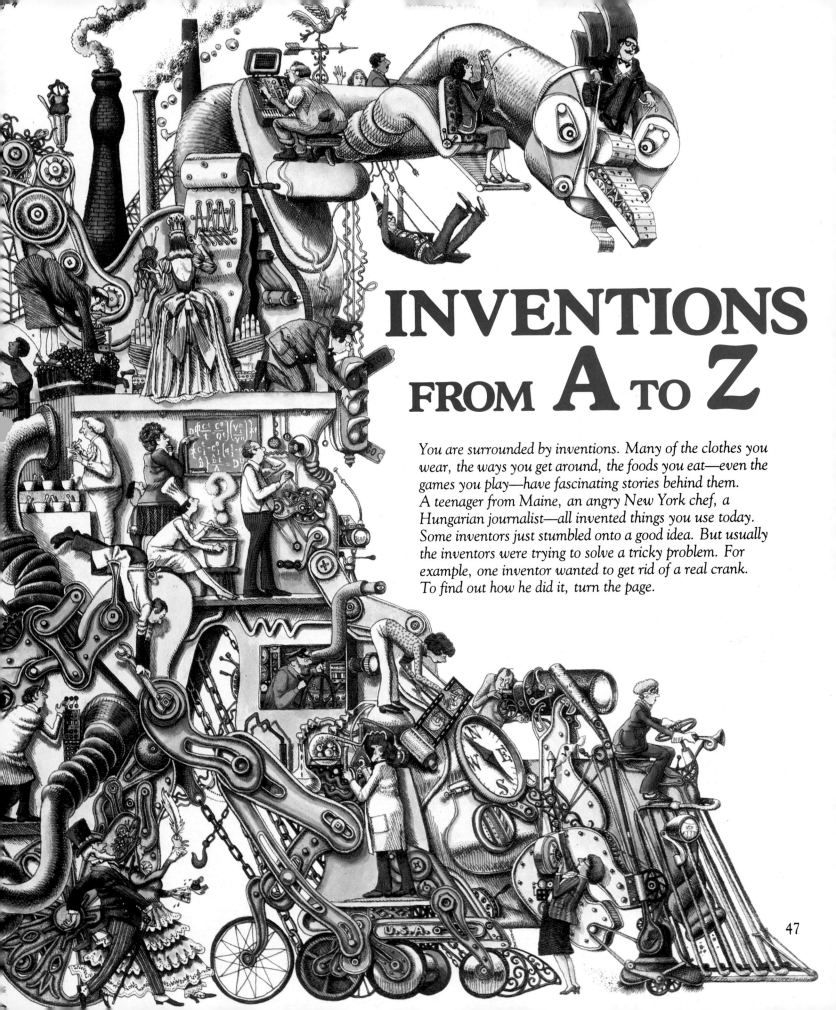

INVENTIONS FROM A TO Z

You are surrounded by inventions. Many of the clothes you wear, the ways you get around, the foods you eat—even the games you play—have fascinating stories behind them. A teenager from Maine, an angry New York chef, a Hungarian journalist—all invented things you use today. Some inventors just stumbled onto a good idea. But usually the inventors were trying to solve a tricky problem. For example, one inventor wanted to get rid of a real crank. To find out how he did it, turn the page.

47

A

AUTOMOBILE SELF-STARTER

Crank . . . pause. *Crank* . . . pause. *Crank* . . . rest. Starting the first automobiles was enough to make anyone cranky. The driver had to bend over in front of the car and turn heavy engine parts with a crank until the engine started (right, top). It was hard work. It took time. And it was dangerous. Sometimes an engine backfired and spun the crank in the opposite direction. Such spins sometimes broke bones and caused other injuries. An inventor named Charles F. Kettering decided that there must be a better way to start a car. In 1910, he and his assistants set to work in a barn in Dayton, Ohio. Working day and night for almost a year, they developed a small, battery-powered motor. It fit under the hood of a car. When the driver pressed a button, motor power—rather than muscle power—started the engine (right). It was quick, easy, and safe.

ALUMINUM FOIL

Aluminum was first used 7,000 years ago, in what is now northern Iraq. There, the clay contained aluminum ore. People beat the clay into thin sheets, then formed it into pottery. The aluminum made the pottery hard and durable. Of course, it wasn't pure aluminum. Not until the 1800s did people actually identify the metal as aluminum and learn how to separate it from the soil. It wasn't until the early 1900s, perhaps in France, that the first foil was pressed out between heavy rollers. Americans first used aluminum foil to make lightweight identification bands for racing pigeons.

Today, people use aluminum foil in dozens of ways. You probably use it as a food wrap—and perhaps as a gift wrap. You may also use it for cooking (left). Foil spreads heat evenly and won't catch on fire. Also, it's convenient. Just pull, rip, wrap—and you're ready.

ASPIRIN

"Take aspirin and stay in bed." That's what your doctor might suggest if you caught the flu or had a bad headache. But 2,000 years ago, in Greece, Rome, and other places, doctors gave out different advice (left). To relieve pain and fever, they prescribed tea made of the bark and leaves of willow trees. The remedy worked—but no one knew exactly why. Then, about 1828, a French scientist named Henri Leroux found the pain-relieving substance in willow. Unfortunately, the substance, called salicin, did not make a good medicine. It had bad side effects.

After that, chemists tried to develop a medicine that would reduce pain without the side effects of salicin. A French scientist came up with just such a compound in 1853—but he didn't realize what he had. The formula for it was soon put aside. In the 1890s, a German chemist named Felix Hofmann took a second look at the compound. He was seeking an effective pain reliever for his father, who suffered from arthritis. Hofmann proved to himself that the substance, acetylsalicylic (uh-SEAT-uhl-sal-uh-SIL-ik) acid, provided just the relief his father needed. He took his evidence to his employers at Friedrich Bayer and Company, a drug manufacturer. They saw the worth of the long-forgotten acid and found an efficient way to mass-produce it. The company gave the tongue twister a new name: aspirin.

Today, aspirin is one of the world's most widely used medicines. Used as directed, it is safe and effective. And it takes up a lot less room than a willow tree.

WILLOW

AQUA–LUNG

There's something fishy about these swimmers: They're able to breathe underwater. They can stay there for as long as an hour and a half. For their underwater adventure, the swimmers can thank a former French naval officer named Jacques-Yves Cousteau. A diver, Cousteau wanted to be able to go deeper and stay down longer than existing breathing equipment allowed. He wanted no hoses attached to the surface. Also, the air supply had to be steady and automatic. In 1942, Cousteau explained what he needed to engineer Émile Gagnan. "Something like this?" Gagnan asked. He held up a small plastic valve he had designed for automobile fuel lines. Using this valve, Cousteau and Gagnan invented the Aqua-Lung. With it, divers could descend to new depths, unconnected to the surface. They could study underwater plants and animals never before seen. Does the name Cousteau sound familiar? You may have watched the inventor as host of a TV series about the undersea world.

B

BATTERY

The time: around 1786. The place: a university in Bologna, Italy. Professor Luigi Galvani sat at an examining table. He was studying the anatomy of the frog. Galvani touched the leg of a dead frog with two rods made of different metals. The rods also touched each other. The leg twitched! Galvani reported that there must be electricity in a frog's muscles. Alessandro Volta, a physics professor at another university, disagreed. He believed the contact between the two metals, and not the frog's leg, produced the electricity.

In 1800, to prove his theory, Volta stacked up many pairs of disks of two unlike metals. Between the pairs of disks, he placed a pad soaked with weak acid. The device gave off a steady electric current. Volta had created the first electric battery.

Since then, scientists have used different materials to develop more efficient batteries. Today, batteries come in many sizes and types for hundreds of purposes (right). Electrical power is measured in units called volts, in honor of the inventor of the battery.

BICYCLE

Bicycles have come a long way since people rode the curious contraption at left. It's a tricycle from the 1800s. Other ancestors of the modern bicycle seem even stranger. The first bicycles, built in the late 1700s, had no pedals. To move them, riders pushed their feet against the ground. In the 1830s, a Scottish blacksmith named Kirkpatrick Macmillan added foot levers called treadles. They worked with an up-and-down motion. He attached them to the rear-wheel axle. The bicycle below had pedals that stayed motionless when the bike coasted. In the 1870s riders perched 5 feet

(1½ m) high on bicycles with huge front wheels and small rear wheels. The riders often toppled off. In the 1880s, safer and more comfortable bicycles began to appear. They had wheels of equal size, chain drives, and, later, air-filled tires (replacing wooden ones). People began using bicycles instead of horses or streetcars. Today, millions of people around the world use bicycles for transportation and for sport (below).

BRAILLE

"I am blind, . . . but if my eyes will not tell me about men and events [and] ideas, I must find another way. . . ." Louis Braille, of Coupvray, in France, wrote those words in 1822, when he was about 13. Braille wanted to read as much and as easily as people who could see. He got an idea from a code once used in the French army. The code consisted of combinations of punch marks in paper. For months on end, Braille worked long into the night. He worked so hard that he sometimes became ill. Finally, at age 15, he developed a system of six raised dots that could be combined in 63 ways. With this system, blind people could read quickly by running their fingertips across the dots (above). The system is now used worldwide. There are Braille wristwatches (right) and even Braille music—all read with feeling.

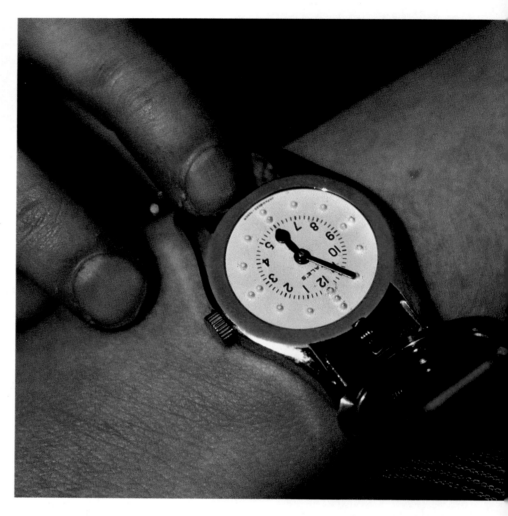

BALLPOINT PEN

In 1935, Hungarian journalist László Biro got tired of the ink blotches his fountain pen made. So he and his brother Georg developed a pen with a rolling ball at the point. The pen wrote without making blotches. The Biros' pen wasn't the first ballpoint, but it was the first one that worked well. The new pens got a big boost during World War II. Pilots needed a pen that would work at high altitudes. Only ballpoints did the job. In 1945, a department store in New York City introduced a ballpoint pen to the public. The store sold 10,000 the first day—at $12.50 each! Today, people buy almost two *billion* ballpoints a year, for as little as 10 cents apiece.

BARBED WIRE

It was county fair time in DeKalb, Illinois, in 1873. Farmer Joseph Glidden was watching a demonstration of a new kind of fence designed to control the movement of cattle. It resembled normal wire fencing, except that spiked wooden strips hung along the wires. *I can improve on that*, Glidden thought. Back home, he twisted short wire barbs, or spikes, onto plain wire. He fastened the barbs with wire strips. The resulting barbed wire was simple and effective. Glidden patented the wire. He also found a way to mass-produce it.

Glidden's wire soon caught on—though not with everyone. Indians called it "devil's rope." Ranchers often cut it down so their cattle could graze freely. Most farmers, however, liked barbed wire. It kept cattle away from their crops. Cattle could break through most wire fences. With barbed wire, they quickly got the point (above). Eventually, ranchers started using barbed wire. With it, they separated the best cattle from the others to produce better breeds. Barbed wire helped railroads keep cattle off the tracks. As a result, the railroads expanded into new territory. Glidden probably didn't realize it at the time, but the few hours he spent twisting wires would help speed the taming of the West.

C

CEMENT AND CONCRETE

Shovel together some chalk and some clay. Heat the mixture to 2,700°F (1,482°C). Add the mineral gypsum. The result is a binding material called portland cement. The ancient Greeks and Romans used a similar cement. The Romans added crushed stone and water to cement to produce concrete, a strong building material. With concrete, they built roads and buildings that stand to this day. When the Roman Empire ended, so did the art of making cement for concrete. For centuries, people tried, but failed, to make good-quality cement. Then, in 1824, an English bricklayer hit on the formula for portland cement. Today, engineers mix portland cement with sand, gravel, and water. This formula makes concrete for highways (right, top) and buildings (right). Strong and watertight, such concrete will be sticking around for years to come.

SUE LEVIN

CEREAL

Will and Dr. John Kellogg were trying to come up with a health food. Will, a business expert, managed John's hospital in Battle Creek, Michigan. They had tried various ways of preparing wheat food after boiling kernels and then rolling them into flat sheets. The reaction: *Ugh!* One day in 1894, the brothers were about to try flattening another batch of boiled wheat. Someone interrupted them. When they returned a few days later, they put the wheat through the rollers. To their surprise, each kernel flattened into a separate flake. Moisture had spread into the kernels, and that had done the trick. Toasted and served with milk, the wheat flakes made a hit with patients. They ate the flakes for breakfast. The Kelloggs packaged their cereal for sale—and started a whole new industry.

COMPASS

Compasses have been pointing people in the right direction for almost a thousand years. The first ones were very simple: a magnetized needle floating on cork or wood in a bowl of water. The Chinese navigated with compasses in the 1100s. That's the earliest recorded use. Over hundreds of years, mariners gradually improved the instrument. They balanced the needle on the point of a pin. They enclosed the compass in a box and added a plate marked with all the compass directions. Today, pocket compasses keep explorers on the right track (left). More complicated, nonmagnetic compasses help ships and airplanes find their way to the four corners of the globe.

CASH REGISTER

Some people called the first cash register a "thief catcher." James Ritty, a café owner in Dayton, Ohio, invented it in 1879 to stop employees from stealing. He also wanted to have an accurate record of each day's sales. Ritty had the idea for the register while on a ship bound for Europe. He noticed a device that counted the turns the ship's propeller made. *Why not invent a machine to count money?* Ritty thought. On his return to Dayton, he did just that. Working with his brother John, he came up with a cash register that looked like a big clock. When an employee punched keys to record a sale, two hands on the face pointed to the amount of the sale. The machine totaled the day's sales. In later models, a cash drawer was added, and numbers popped up with each sale (right). A bell attracted attention. No longer could employees slip money into their pockets unnoticed. Before long, the ring of the cash register was a familiar sound in stores throughout the country.

D

DYE

For more than 5,000 years, people have brightened their lives with color. During most of this time, people made dyes from plants, animals, and earth. But natural dyes varied in shade from batch to batch and were difficult to make. Not until 1856 was the chemical-dye industry born—and that was by accident. In England, William Perkin, 18, was trying to make the chemical quinine from coal tar. All he got was a sticky black mess. Curious, Perkin experimented with the goo, eventually creating a purplish liquid. When silk was dipped into the liquid, the silk turned purple. Further experiments produced a rainbow of colors. Perkin went on to start the chemical-dye industry. Chemical dyes (below) soon replaced natural ones. They cost less, and the colors were less variable. Yarns (left) show a handful of the thousands of shades chemical dyes provide.

DYNAMITE

"Leave it alone!" warned the man who in 1846 invented the explosive nitroglycerin (NYE-truh-GLIS-uh-run). He feared his own invention. But the oily liquid was used in demolition work anyway. It sometimes exploded unexpectedly, killing workers.

Another inventor, Alfred Nobel, made nitroglycerin in his plant in Sweden. When an explosion in the plant killed his younger brother, Nobel resolved to tame

nitroglycerin. After many failures, he tried combining the liquid with a chalky soil and shaping the mixture into a stick. Being careful not to endanger anyone, he then tried to make the stick explode. He used both fire and force. Nothing happened. Not until Nobel attached a device called a blasting cap and triggered an explosion in the cap did the stick explode.

Nobel patented the stick in 1867 under the name dynamite. The word comes from a Greek word meaning "power." Dynamite takes much of the danger out of big demolition jobs, such as the destruction of this old hotel in Tampa, Florida.

DENTURES

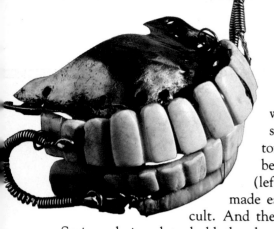

Did you ever wonder why portraits never show George Washington smiling? It could be because of his dentures (left). They hurt. They made eating and talking difficult. And they didn't stay in place. Springs designed to hold the dentures in place actually pushed the teeth forward. If Washington was tight-lipped, it was probably to prevent his teeth from popping out.

The first false teeth were made of ivory, bone, gold, or human teeth. People in Italy used them as many as 2,500 years ago. Not until the late 1700s did dentists start making dentures from porcelain. Today's dentures (right), usually made of plastic, are custom-molded to the shape of the wearer's mouth. They are the most comfortable and lifelike ever. Washington might have given his eyeteeth for such a set.

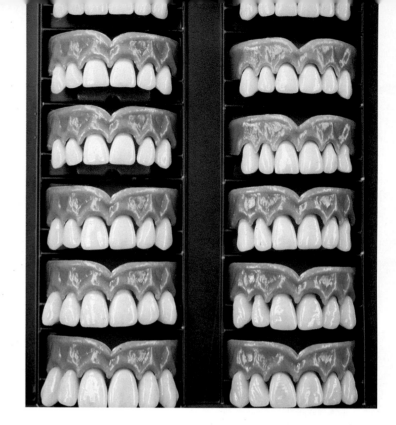

EARMUFFS

Chester Greenwood's ears were the talk of the town. Whenever the temperature plunged below freezing, they turned chalky white . . . then bright red . . . and finally deep blue. This embarrassed Chester. It hurt, too.

One frosty day in 1873, Chester, 15, was ice-skating on a pond near his home in Farmington, Maine. His ears did their usual routine. This time, he decided to do something about it. He ran home and twisted some wire into two loops.

He asked his grandmother to sew cloth onto them. He dashed back to the pond and put the muffs over his ears. They worked! Chester's ears stayed warm. Later, Chester added a spring that fit over his head and held the muffs in place.

Soon Chester's Champion Ear Protectors became the talk of the town. Everybody wanted a pair. In 1877, at the age of 18, Chester received a patent for his invention. He opened a factory to manufacture the earmuffs and sold millions. Now every year on the first day of winter, the citizens of Farmington celebrate Chester Greenwood Day.

EYEGLASSES

For a person who wore eyeglasses before the 1700s, it helped to have a big nose. Eyeglasses first appeared in the late 1200s, in Italy. They consisted of quartz lenses and a frame. The frame held the lenses together, but it did not hold them in place. People had to balance the glasses on the nose or hold them with their hands. It wasn't until the 1720s that an English optician came up with a better way to hold eyeglasses in place. He invented sidepieces that rested on the ears. It took a while for this idea to catch on. Before it did, spectacles were often quite a spectacle (below).

As eyeglass frames improved, so did the lenses. Early lenses curved only outward. They helped farsighted people —those who couldn't see things close up. Eyeglasses for nearsighted people weren't invented until around 1500. They had lenses that curved inward. In the late 1700s, Benjamin Franklin combined the two kinds of lenses to make the first bifocals. They helped people who had both vision problems.

At first, finding the right eyeglass was a matter of trial and error. A customer would try on a series of standard lenses until he found the ones that seemed to work best. In time, opticians learned to grind lenses for individual needs. Today, machines grind prescription lenses to exact measurements. Eyeglasses correct many vision problems. For millions of people, they are like a new pair of eyes.

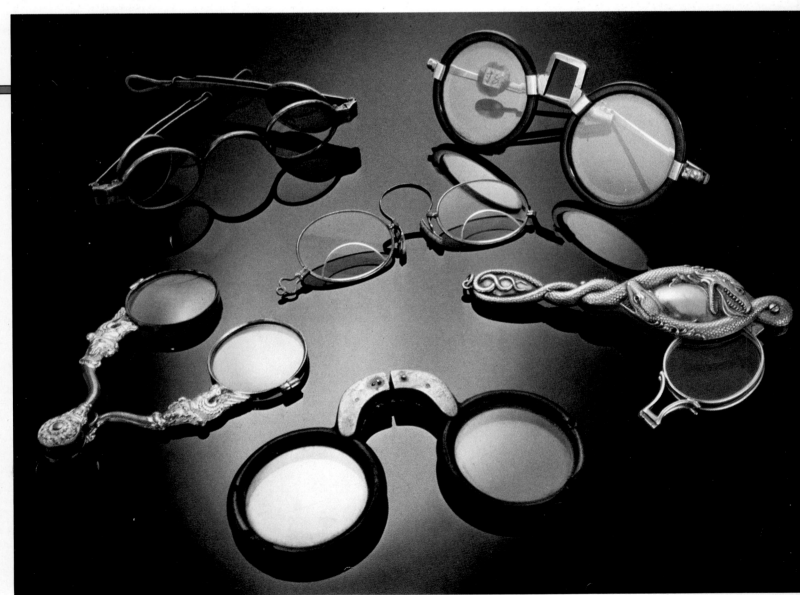

ELEVATOR

A bearded man mounted a platform at a fair in New York City in 1854. Another man pulled a rope. The platform rose high above the crowd. "Cut the rope!" cried the bearded man. The assistant did as he was told. The crowd gasped. The platform jerked—then stopped.

The bearded man, Elisha Otis, was demonstrating his invention, the safety elevator. When the rope was cut, a heavy spring on the platform caught on notched side rails. This prevented the platform from crashing. Unlike hoists used to lift heavy objects, the elevator was safe for people to ride.

A store in New York City installed the first passenger elevator in 1857. It was steam driven and traveled five stories. Water pressure powered elevators built later in the 1800s (below). During the 1900s, electric elevators took over. Now elevators whisk people up skyscrapers as high as 110 stories. Some even have a view (right). Elevators make modern, high-rise cities possible—and give millions of people a lift.

FROZEN AND FREEZE–DRIED FOOD

Next time you enjoy strawberry shortcake in midwinter, thank an American fur trader named Clarence Birdseye. He invented modern frozen foods. In 1914–17, Birdseye lived among Eskimos in Labrador, in Canada. There, he watched the people preserve fish and meat by freezing them outdoors in the cold, dry northern air. Months later, the Eskimos would thaw and cook the food. It was tender, and it tasted fresh. Birdseye returned to the United States with an idea. In Gloucester, Massachusetts, he perfected a quick-freezing method and began selling packaged frozen food. Now people could eat seasonal foods—such as strawberries—year round. Birdseye made a fortune. His idea led to the vast variety of frozen foods we use today (above). Later inventors found a way to remove most of the water from frozen foods. This process, called freeze-drying, produces a lightweight food (left) that can be stored at room temperature. Adding water to the food gives it back its original shape and color. Freeze-dried foods are carried by all sorts of adventurers, from backpackers to astronauts.

FIREWORKS

You probably think of fireworks as being as American as the Fourth of July. No Independence Day celebration would be complete without a loud and splashy display, such as this one above New York City. Actually, fireworks go back a long way before our nation won its independence. The Chinese probably made the first fireworks about a thousand years ago. They found they could produce explosions and fountains of fire by lighting bamboo tubes packed with explosive powder. For the Chinese, fireworks had—and still have—a serious purpose: scaring away evil spirits. The art of firework making traveled west with European traders. The Europeans added color to the bursts by mixing chemicals with the powder. Today, firework makers in many countries compete to create ever more spectacular displays.

FLUORESCENT LIGHTING

In 1602, an Italian cobbler noticed a rock that glowed in the dark. *Does it glow because it contains gold?* he wondered. To his disappointment, it did not. But the discovery led experimenters to find the cause of the glow—and that in turn led to the invention of fluorescent (flur-ES-uhnt) lighting. Some minerals, it was found, contain phosphorescent (FAHS-fuh-RES-uhnt) or fluorescent substances. Both substances react to certain forms of energy by giving off their own light. Could such material be used to provide an efficient form of home lighting? About 1859, French scientist Alexandre Edmond Becquerel decided to find out. He coated the inside of a glass tube with a fluorescent substance. Then he sent an electric charge through the tube. It was the first attempt at a fluorescent lamp. About 80 years passed before the invention was perfected. In the United States today, fluorescent tubes (right) outsell light bulbs. They are used mostly in schools, offices, and factories. Their light is cooler, softer, and cheaper than ordinary electric light.

G

GLUE

You've probably seen pictures of them: paintings of animals brushed onto cave walls by people thousands of years ago. If so, you've seen one of the earliest uses of glues. Prehistoric artists mixed glues with coloring to make the paints for their cave murals. For the glue, they used raw eggs, dried blood, and sticky juices from plants and insects. Later, the Egyptians and other people learned to make stronger glues by boiling animal bones and hides.

For a long time, glues stayed much the same. Then, in the early 1900s, chemists started adding synthetic substances for extra strength. In recent years, chemists have developed glues made entirely of synthetic substances. Multipurpose glues stick to many different kinds of surfaces (left). "Super glues" can hold firm against a pull of two *tons*. Epoxy glues resist moisture and high temperatures. With the wide variety to choose from today, there's no reason to get stuck with the wrong glue.

GLASS

Scientists believe that people began using glass about 75,000 years ago. The glass was obsidian (ub-SID-ee-un), a kind formed by volcanic action. From this natural glass, people chipped spearheads, knives, and razors. The first glass made by people appeared in the Middle East roughly 3,500 years ago. The invention probably came about by accident. Workers may have noticed glass as a by-product of some manufacturing process that used fire. About 2,000 years ago, people learned to shape bottles and other containers by blowing through a tube dipped into molten, or melted, glass.

Today, we sometimes seem to live in a world of glass (right). The formula for some kinds of glass remains about the same as in ancient times: sand, soda, and the mineral lime. Other substances may be added for strength or color. The mixture is heated until it melts and the ingredients blend. Machines mold glass quickly, cheaply, and uniformly. Some jobs, however, call for the skills of a professional glassblower. Glassblowers create such things as complicated neon signs and delicate crystal ware.

GEARS

Wheels with interlocking teeth, gears help run almost all our machines—from watches to bulldozers. Gears transfer motion from one machine part to another. They speed up or slow down a machine, as desired. They also change the direction of motion. The Chinese may have used gears 5,000 years ago. The Egyptians and Babylonians probably began using gears in clocks and in lifting equipment 3,000 years ago. Ever since, gears have helped replace muscle power with machine power. Without them, much of our world would grind to a halt.

64

H HEARING AID

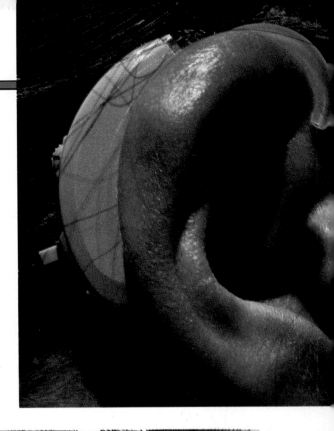

As you read on page 7, Alexander Graham Bell wanted to help the deaf. He spent years trying to develop communication devices for them. Although he never actually invented a hearing aid, his work was not wasted. The knowledge he gained in his experiments inspired him to invent the telephone. In turn, the telephone inspired another American inventor, Miller Hutchison, of New York City, to develop a hearing aid. It occurred to Hutchison that the telephone, changed in certain ways, could help the deaf. In 1902, Hutchison patented a battery-powered hearing aid. It worked much like a telephone. First it changed sounds into electrical signals. Then it amplified the signals and changed them back to sounds that were louder than the original ones. Soon, electric hearing aids had replaced ear trumpets (below), which for centuries had helped people who had hearing problems. Hutchison's hearing aid was large and bulky. With the development of transistors and coin-size batteries, hearing aids have become miniaturized. One popular model (right) tucks behind the ear, making it barely noticeable.

HORSESHOE

You wouldn't think of going on a hike without sturdy shoes to protect your feet. A hardworking horse needs the same protection. The Romans learned this 2,000 years ago. Roman soldiers wore heavy armor. Their horses sometimes had to carry them and their equipment long distances over rough terrain. Without shoes, the horses' hooves wore down. Eventually, they splintered, like the hoof above. Worn hooves could cause a horse pain and make it go lame. To prevent this, the

Romans fitted metal shoes over their horses' hooves. In the cartoon above, the horse at left wears shoes; the other horse doesn't. The Romans called their horseshoes *hipposandals.* (*Hippos* is the Greek word for "horse.") The shoes absorbed shocks and gave the horse a better grip on the ground. By about A.D. 900, metal horseshoes nailed to the hoof came into use. They have remained much the same ever since.

I INCUBATOR

Thousands of years ago, the Egyptians hatched an idea that's still worth clucking about. To increase their supply of chickens, they came up with the incubator. This device took the place of mother hens in the hatching of eggs. It freed the hens to continue laying. The Egyptian incubator was a brick building warmed inside by open fires burning on shelves. Attendants placed eggs along the floor. They turned the eggs to warm them evenly. About the same time, the Chinese also developed incubators. One type was warmed by fire. Heat released by decaying animal droppings warmed another type. A French inventor, Antoine Ferchault de Réaumur, introduced the incubator to Europe around 1750. A wood stove warmed it. Today, in the U. S., most farmers use electrically heated incubators that turn the eggs automatically. Incubators help ensure a plentiful supply of eggs and chickens.

ICE CREAM

The average American eats several gallons of ice cream a year. But not too long ago, only the wealthy could afford frozen desserts. One of the first people to enjoy such treats was the Roman ruler Nero. He lived nearly 2,000 years ago. Since there were no ice-making machines then, Nero had slaves bring him mountain snow. A few centuries later, wealthy Asians enjoyed a flavored-ice dish. Marco Polo brought the recipe to Europe around 1300. Europeans probably churned the first true ice *cream* around 1600. The average person, however, rarely tasted the dessert until the early 1800s. That's when commercial icehouses appeared. Ice cut from frozen lakes was shipped to these houses and preserved through the summer. Shops could make ice cream cheaply nearly anytime. Later, a New Jersey woman named Nancy Johnson invented a home ice-cream maker. For cones, people can thank a waffle vendor at the 1904 St. Louis World's Fair. When a neighboring ice-cream stand ran out of dishes, so the story goes, he rolled waffles into cones to hold the treat. Cones were a hit—and that's the straight scoop.

SUE LEVIN

INK

If you want to write to a friend, you probably just reach for a pen. But writing wasn't always so easy. Until a few thousand years ago, it was real work. People had to carve their messages onto tablets of wax or soft clay. The first inks appeared about 4,500 years ago in China and Egypt. These inks were mixtures mostly of soot, water, and plant material. Some permanent inks today use much the same formula. Inks are specially made to fit a variety of needs. Copyists use permanent inks to make lasting documents, such as this copy of an ancient Hebrew manuscript (right). Some inks, such as those used for marking needlework, are made to wash out easily. There are inks that glow in the dark. The ink used in printing pages like this one is thicker than the ink you use for writing. Things that contain ink are all around you. It's an invention that clearly has left its mark.

J

JEANS

In 1847, a teenager left his home in Bavaria, in what is now West Germany, to start a new life in America. He carried little more than a dream of riches. Today, people everywhere know his name: Levi Strauss.

Soon after Strauss arrived in the United States, gold was discovered in California. Strauss joined the thousands seeking their fortunes there. He took along rolls of canvas to sell to miners as a material for tents and wagon covers. But miners needed sturdy trousers even more, he soon realized. Strauss began stitching trousers from his canvas. Soon, all the miners wanted "those pants of Levi's." After a time, Strauss switched from canvas to strong but softer cotton denim. Copper rivets were added to strengthen the pockets. People started calling the product jeans. The word was a rough pronunciation of Genoa, an Italian city where denimlike fabric was made. Today's Levi's jeans are much the same as the originals. An early symbol of their toughness remains a trademark: two horses straining to pull a pair of Levi's jeans apart.

JET ENGINE

In 1929, Frank Whittle was a 22-year-old officer in Britain's Royal Air Force. He'd been working on an idea: a new way to power aircraft. His idea, the jet engine, would do away with rods and spark plugs and other parts of the piston engine. The action of the engine expelling gas under high pressure would push a plane forward. The jet engine would enable aircraft to fly at much greater speeds than were possible with the piston engine. Whittle took his idea to the Air Ministry. The ministry rejected it. Knowing that the idea was sound, Whittle patented his design on his own in 1930. But it was the Germans who, in 1939, built and flew the first jet plane. By the end of World War II, both the Germans and the British were using jets. Today, jet engines (right) power airliners (above). Jet engines also make course corrections in orbiting space shuttles. And what of Whittle? After people realized the importance of his invention, the King of England knighted him.

JIGSAW PUZZLE

Around 1760, an Englishman named John Spilsbury thought that children might learn their geography more easily if the subject were turned into a game. Spilsbury painted slabs of wood as maps of various regions. Then he cut the wood along boundary lines—the first jigsaw puzzles. Spilsbury's idea led to the puzzles that are popular today (above). There's a jigsaw puzzle for every level of skill. Puzzles for beginners contain just a few pieces. Advanced puzzle solvers may have a fit trying to fit together the larger ones—some with 5,000 pieces!

JUICE CONCENTRATE

Every morning, millions of people wake up to frozen juice that tastes nearly as natural as freshly squeezed juice. Juice concentrate makes the fresh taste possible. Before the mid-1940s, orange juice, for example, came in two forms: fresh (when oranges were available) and canned. Canned juice did not taste fresh. That caused experimenters in Florida to try to find a way to preserve fresh taste. They hit on a method still used today. In an airless tank, they evaporated most of the water from orange juice. To the syrupy liquid remaining, they added a bit of fresh juice for natural appearance and taste. They then froze the mixture. The resulting concentrate is so handy and so fresh tasting that it far outsells freshly squeezed juice—even in Florida.

100% Orange Juice
PURE FROZEN CONCENTRATE

NET 12 FL. OZ. (354ml)

MAKES 1½ QUARTS

KEEP FROZEN

K

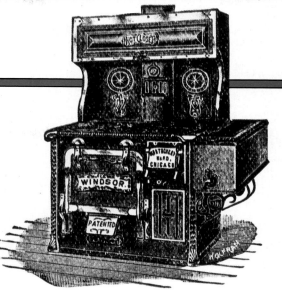

KITCHEN STOVE

For centuries, cooking was something to get heated up about. People cooked food in their fireplaces (left). It was difficult to control the flames, impossible to direct them. Not until the 1700s was the kitchen stove introduced. Early models burned wood or coal. Homemakers found these stoves (above) more convenient than the fireplace, but they still had trouble controlling the heat. The gas stove, first made in England in the mid-1800s, solved that problem. A turn of the knob could adjust the flame. Electric stoves became popular in the late 1920s, when electricity became cheap. In recent years, another type of cooking device has caught on. It's the microwave oven. Microwaves—a kind of radio wave—cook food in a fraction of the time needed by gas or electricity.

KNIFE

For Stone Age people, it came down to survival. They needed tools to kill and skin animals for food, clothing, and shelter. They found that sharp stones could do the job. Hundreds of thousands of years ago, scientists believe, people of the Stone Age made hand axes from rock. Later, pounding stone against stone, they chipped off flakes, then sharpened them into the first knife blades. The stone blades broke easily. Sturdier ones were made after the discovery of metals. The first metal used was copper, around 5000 B.C. Bronze, which is stronger, came into use 2,000 years later. Now most knives have blades of steel. Pocketknives (right) may have several tools tucked into one handle. Such knives are a miniature tool shop and wilderness outfitter combined in one palm-size package.

KNITTING MACHINE

One day, so the story goes, a 16th-century Englishman named William Lee decided that his wife was working too hard. She spent long hours knitting by hand. The process had changed little in thousands of years. With knitting needles, Mrs. Lee made a loop, then pulled another loop through the first one. She repeated the process over and over. Perhaps, Lee thought, he could save his wife some work. Lee developed a frame containing many needles and hooks—the first knitting machine. It knitted a long row of loops in one simple action. You can see a modern version of Lee's home knitting machine at right. The invention led eventually to huge, high-speed factory knitting machines.

KNOTS

Why knot? Why *not!* Properly tied, a knot can help you do many things. One kind, the bowknot, keeps your shoes on your feet. Another, the square knot, secures a package for mailing. The bowline (BO-lin) will neither slip nor jam. It ties a rope to a limb (left) for swinging or climbing.

Scientists think people may have tied the first knots hundreds of thousands of years ago. Perhaps the first knots, tied with vine, fastened stone axheads to handles. Later, knots helped bind logs together as rafts.

Sailors have invented dozens of knots for different purposes. Some knots join ropes together. Others tie a ship to a pier or help hoist cargo. Some knots are designed strictly for show. They help a ship look shipshape.

L

LAWN MOWER

For centuries, a well-trimmed lawn was considered a luxury. Mowing a large lawn often required hours of work with a scythe (right, top). Some people even used grazing animals to trim their lawns.

An Englishman named Edwin Budding thought there must be a better way to cut grass. Budding was an engineer in a textile mill. In 1830, borrowing an idea from a machine that trimmed fabric, he made a reel mower (right, middle). Blades attached to a revolving cylinder cut the grass. Budding's advertisements proclaimed, "Country gentlemen may find [that using] my machine [provides] an amusing, useful, and healthy exercise." Others had invented grass-cutting machines, but Budding's was the first one that worked well.

In the early 1900s, inventors started attaching gasoline motors to reel mowers. They used motors designed for motorcycles and washing machines.

In the 1940s, inventors came up with a new type of power mower, the rotary mower (right, bottom). Instead of several blades on a reel, the rotary mower has a single blade that spins horizontally under a safety hood.

When you see a power mower these days, chances are it's a rotary mower. Many people still use a push mower, however. Its basic design has hardly changed since Budding made his model more than 150 years ago.

LIGHT BULB

Thomas Edison invented the electric light bulb, right? Wrong—people had experimented with light bulbs at least 70 years before Edison did. Edison invented and manufactured the first *practical* light bulb. He also invented the entire electric-power system. Homes in his time did not have electricity. Without power, a light bulb would have been useless. Edison designed power plants that would generate electricity and send it through wires into homes. He also invented special electrical switches, meters, and circuits.

As for the light bulb, Edison's great contribution was finding a material that would glow for a long time before it burned up. (If you have read page 6, you already know what that material was.) Edison began testing his bulb on October 19, 1879. It glowed for 40 hours. Modern lighting was born!

LOCK

For at least 4,000 years, people have been using locks to foil thieves. The Egyptians designed the oldest key-operated lock yet found. The pegged wooden key was more than a foot (1/3 m) long. When inserted into a slot, the pegs lifted pins inside the lock and opened it. Over the centuries, locksmithing became a respected craft. It took skill and inventiveness to design devices that would outwit lock pickers. In the 1860s, an American inventor named Linus Yale, Jr., continued work on an idea of his father's. He patented a pin-tumbler cylinder lock. It combined the features of several locks, including the pins of the Egyptian design. It's the most common door lock in use today. Now inventors are designing electronic locks that open at the sound of a particular voice or at the touch of a particular hand.

LASER

Zap! A narrow, brilliant beam of light streaks into the sky, toward a camera on the surface of the moon. Scientists are experimenting to find out how well the camera detects light from earth. But this is not ordinary light. It's laser light. It is highly concentrated, and it can be made much more powerful than ordinary light.

You could trace the laser's beginning to a park bench in Washington, D.C. There, one spring dawn in 1951, physicist Charles H. Townes came up with an idea for a maser. The maser would amplify and beam invisible microwaves.

Townes soon built a working maser. After that, the race was on to build a laser, for amplifying and beaming light waves. In 1960, American physicist Theodore H. Maiman won the race. Those who viewed demonstrations of the laser felt it could be useful. They just weren't sure how.

Since then, the laser has become an important tool that can do a variety of jobs. Lasers pierce holes in objects ranging from baby-bottle nipples to diamonds. In the hands of surgeons, weak beams from a laser painlessly seal torn tissue inside the human eye. Laser beams, rather than wires, may someday carry most telephone traffic.

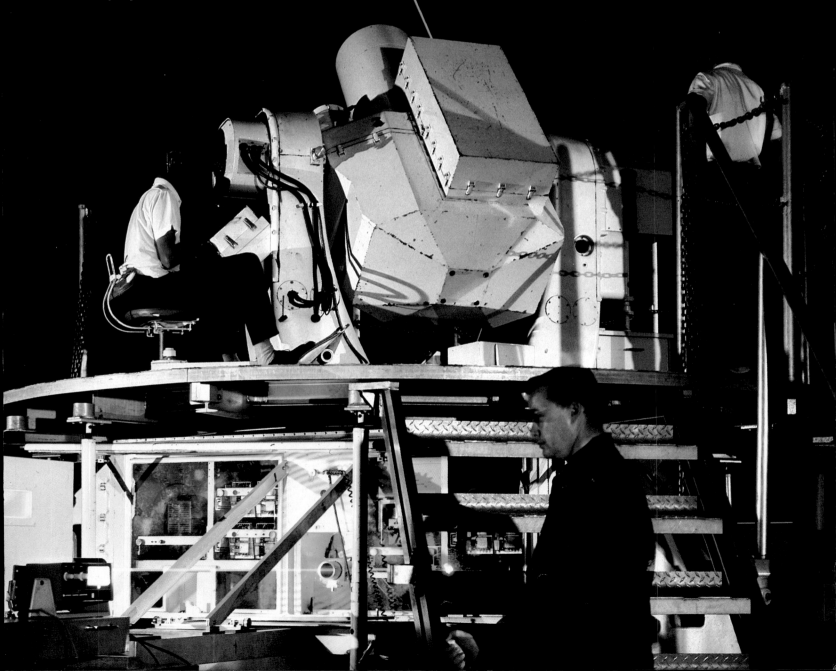

M

MICROSCOPE

People began using glass lenses to improve vision about 1300. Nearly 300 years later, a Dutch family, the Janssens, made an important discovery. They put one lens above another in a tube. Used together, the lenses had a multiplying effect. But such microscopes, called compound microscopes, did not immediately catch on.

In the 1660s, a Dutchman named Anton Van Leeuwenhoek began using microscopes for scientific purposes. He became famous for his detailed descriptions of bacteria and one-celled animals.

Microscopes opened up whole new worlds for people to examine. Much of what we know today in such fields as medicine and biology is based on discoveries made through the microscope.

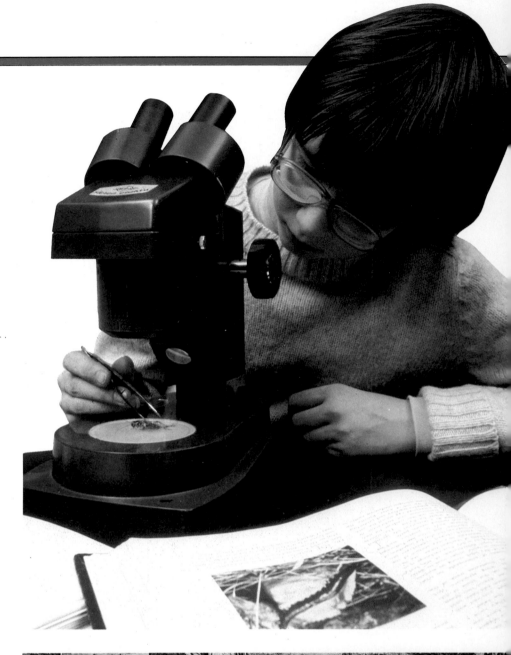

MOVABLE TYPE

You can imagine what a job it would be if you had to copy this page by hand. For centuries, however, that's how people made books. With great care, they hand-copied books, letter by letter. It was a slow and expensive process. Only the rich owned books.

In the mid-1400s, Johann Gutenberg, a German metalworker, discovered a way to make copies of books much faster than by writing. He invented a method of casting letters in metal, setting them in lines, and printing them. Actually, the Chinese had done much the same thing around 1040. But written Chinese requires thousands of symbols. Printing was not very practical for that language. An alphabet is much shorter. Movable type worked well for Gutenberg. He built a press (right) and printed a large Bible.

Printing soon spread throughout Europe. No longer were books, and the information they held, for only the wealthy few.

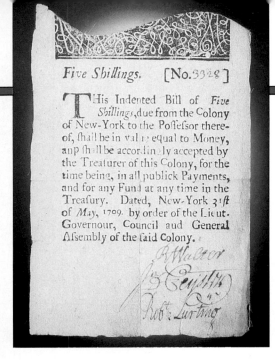

Five Shillings. [No. 3328]

THIS Indented Bill of *Five Shillings*, due from the Colony of New-York to the Poffeffor thereof, fhall be in value equal to Money, and fhall be accordingly accepted by the Treafurer of this Colony, for the time being, in all publick Payments, and for any Fund at any time in the Treafury. Dated, New-York 31ft of *May*, 1709. by order of the Lieut. Governour, Council and General Affembly of the faid Colony.

long before the United States became independent. The colony of New York issued a five-shilling note (left) in 1709. Other types of cash shown here are a $20 gold piece (above), a $1 gold piece (above, right), stone money (right) used on the Pacific island of Yap, and a $100,000 bill (below). Credit cards (bottom) began substituting for folding and jingling money in the 1960s. Today, many people prefer saying "Charge it!" to carrying cash.

MONEY

When you receive your allowance or earn money from chores or baby-sitting, you feel good. You know that you'll be able to exchange the coins and pieces of paper for snacks, records, clothes—anything you can afford to buy.

Money has been around for nearly as long as people have had goods or services to exchange. But it hasn't always come in the form of coins and bills. Salt was once used as money; so were furs, grains, and cloth. Some American colonists used tobacco as money. American Indians traded with strings of beads called wampum. In Iceland a few hundred years ago, the going price for a pair of women's shoes was three dried fish.

Hauling a cartful of fish or leading an ox to the store was inconvenient, however. People needed money that was long lasting, easy to carry, and accepted by everyone. Metal filled all the requirements. About 2500 B.C., the Egyptians began using metal rings as money. The ancient kingdom of Lydia issued what were probably the first state-made coins about 600 B.C.

The Chinese probably invented paper money. Italian explorer Marco Polo saw Chinese people trading with paper money in the 1200s. However, no one knows how much earlier they actually began using it.

In America, people used paper money

N

NAIL

Whap!—missed again! You know how it is with nails. Sometimes you bend one. You throw it out and try again. After all, it's only a nail. In ancient times, people considered nails to be valuable. About 5,000 years ago, people in the Middle East made what were perhaps the first nails. Nails were crafted by hand—one by one. Craftsmen heated metal to soften it, then pounded it into shape. Nails continued to be mostly handmade for thousands of years. About 1777, a Rhode Islander named Jeremiah Wilkinson invented a machine that cut nails from sheets of cold iron. In the mid-1800s, the first machine for making nails from wire was built. Today, nail production is so fast and so cheap that bending a nail is merely a nuisance, not a big loss.

NEEDLE

When a Stone Age hunter killed an animal, it provided more than just food. Animal skins gave warmth. Bones became punching tools and needles. Sinew—stringy connective tissue—served as thread. Before they had needles with eyes, people sewed skins together somewhat as you lace a shoe. They threaded sinew through holes they had punched with a sliver of bone. Later, people learned to carve small hooks into the sliver to pull the sinew. Finally, 15,000 years ago—perhaps longer—someone thought to make a hole in the sliver, and the needle as we know it came into use.

OUTBOARD MOTOR

It was a hot summer day in Milwaukee, Wisconsin, in 1907. Ole Evinrude, a Norwegian-born American, had rowed his sweetheart, Bessie, to an island for a picnic. Suddenly, so the story goes, Bessie wanted ice cream. Eager to please, Evinrude rowed the 2 miles (3 km) back to shore and fetched the ice cream. It melted on the slow row back. *Drat!* thought Evinrude. *There must be a faster way to move a rowboat through the water.* In his workshop, he built an outboard motor—after marrying Bessie. The couple went into business. Other inventors had built boat motors earlier, but Evinrude's design was the most commercially and mechanically successful.

More than eight million boats now have outboard motors. The boats haul fishermen, carry police on patrol, tow water-skiers—and even deliver ice cream before it melts.

OIL LUBRICATOR

Here's the real McCoy—Elijah McCoy, inventor of the oil lubricator. McCoy was born in Canada, the son of runaway slaves. He studied engineering in Scotland and later took a job as a fireman and oilman for a railroad in Michigan.

At regular intervals, the trains had to stop so the engines could be oiled. The crew would squirt oil between the engine's moving parts. Without oil, the parts would rub together until they overheated. The entire train might grind to a halt.

To McCoy, stopping a train for oiling seemed to be a waste of time and money. In 1872, he created a device he called a lubricator. It was designed to oil engine parts automatically while they moved.

Railroad workers liked the device. It caught the attention of other machinists, and McCoy designed lubricators for their needs as well. People buying machines began to insist that they come equipped only with McCoy lubricators. They wanted "the real McCoy"—or no sale.

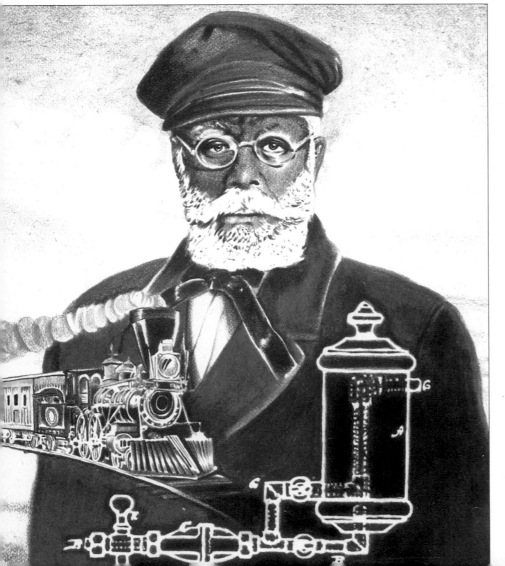

79

P

PAPER

People have been writing for more than 5,000 years, but not always on paper. Before they had paper, they wrote on such material as bones and clay. Later, papyrus, a paperlike material made from plant strips, came into use. The Chinese made the first true paper around A.D. 100. They mixed rags and plant fibers with water, pounded them to a pulp, and pressed out the liquid. When the pulp dried, a sheet of paper remained. The art of papermaking eventually spread to other regions. Until the early 1800s, craftsmen used rags to make paper piece by piece. Then machines that could mass-produce paper came on the scene. Rags soon became scarce. In the mid-1800s, inventors developed methods of making paper from wood pulp. Today, people use paper in hundreds of products. About half of all the paper manufactured in the U. S. is used for packaging.

PLOW

Historians consider the plow to be one of the most important inventions of all time. By making farming practical, the plow helped change the course of civilization. People could grow food instead of hunting and gathering it. People in the Middle East first used the plow at least 6,000 years ago. It was a simple forked stick, pulled by a person. About a thousand years later, oxen were first used to pull plows. As the plow spread to other regions, people improved on it to make it dig deeper and faster. In the U. S. today, a few farmers use simple horse-drawn plows (left). On most farms (above), tractors pull huge plows. The plows prepare the soil, helping farmers grow food for millions of people.

PLYWOOD

You could think of plywood as a kind of sandwich (below). It's made up of layers of wood glued together. Each layer is called a ply or a veneer. The grain in one ply usually runs opposite to the grain in the next. This makes the piece of plywood stronger and helps it resist warping, or bending out of shape.

The ancient Egyptians used veneers of fine wood as attractive coverings for lower quality wood. But plywood as we know it didn't appear until around 1900. Machines in plywood mills peel off long, thin ribbons of wood from logs (above). Other machines cut the wood to size, apply glue, and press layers together.

At first, plywood could be used only inside—for floors, doors, cabinets, and walls. With the development of waterproof glue, plywood has been used to construct buildings (left), airplanes, and boats.

81

POTATO CHIPS

One day in 1853, a proud chef decided to punish a critical customer. The result: one of America's favorite snacks.

The chef, George Crum, worked at a restaurant in Saratoga Springs, New York. The customer had just turned his nose up at Crum's French fries. "Too thick and soggy," the customer had complained. "Not salty enough." Furious, Crum cut a potato into paper-thin slices. He soaked the slices in ice water for 30 minutes. Then he fried them until they were brown and crisp. As a final touch, he salted them heavily. Crum served the chips, sure that the customer would hate them. The customer took a bite. *Crunch.* A smile spread across his face. He loved them!

Soon, people all over town were asking for Crum's "Saratoga chips." People in other parts of the country began making them. Today, you can munch on smooth potato chips or crinkly ones (right). You can even try a variety of flavors. The average American eats about 4 pounds (2 kg) of chips a year—and seems to enjoy every crunch.

Q

QUARTZ WATCH

In 1880, a French scientist discovered something unusual about the mineral quartz. When it's cut a certain way and electricity is passed through it, quartz oscillates—moves back and forth. More than that, it oscillates at a constant rate. Clockmakers first used quartz in the 1920s, with two results: accuracy and silence. Quartz oscillators replaced the moving parts that went *tick-tock.* Development of the microchip made quartz practical for watches. The first quartz wristwatches appeared in 1969. In a quartz watch, power from a battery or a solar cell keeps the quartz oscillating inside a capsule. A capsule is shown in red at left. Two clamps hold it. A microchip translates the oscillations into one-second pulses—and time goes quietly on.

R
ROLLER
SKATES

One day in 1760, Joseph Merlin, a Belgian, dressed for a costume ball. He put on his latest invention, a pair of wheeled shoes. But they were hard to steer. Merlin crashed into a large mirror, smashing it. In 1863, an inventor found a way to make skates steerable. James Plimpton, of Medfield, Massachusetts, put rubber cushions between the foot plates and the axles. The cushions allowed slight motion between the two parts. By shifting his weight, a skater could use that motion to steer. Roller skating swept America and Europe. Many people used skates like the one below, made in 1882. Plastic wheels give the colorful modern skates above a smooth, whisper-quiet ride. In the U. S. today, more than 25 million skaters whirl around more than 4,000 rinks. Millions more keep the sport rolling along on sidewalks (right).

READY–MADE CLOTHES

Two hundred years ago, few clothing stores existed. Most women made their families' clothes by hand. In the early 1800s, a few small factories began making ready-to-wear clothes. But the clothes neither fitted well nor looked good. Most people wouldn't buy them.

A machine and a war changed all that. In 1851, American inventor Isaac Singer designed and marketed a practical sewing machine. (It used a special needle, patented earlier by another American, Elias Howe.) Ten years later, the Civil War broke out. Thousands of soldiers needed uniforms—fast.

Factories installed sewing machines, mostly Singers, to speed production. Manufacturers worked out standard sizes to fit most men. After the war, factories continued to produce clothes cut to standard sizes. As the quality improved, people began to buy.

Today, in large manufacturing plants, workers cut, stitch, and press clothes and hang them on racks (above, left). The racks may be transported within a busy fashion district in a large city (above, right). They may end up in a department store (below). There, you can choose clothes right off the rack that fit well.

RUBBER

Sixteenth-century Spanish explorers in South America found Indians playing games with balls made from the sap of a tree. The sap—latex—was elastic and waterproof. It could be molded into any shape. In the late 1700s, an English chemist, Joseph Priestley, noticed that it rubbed pencil marks off paper. In time, the material was named rubber. Rubber became soft and sticky in heat, and hard and brittle in cold. In 1839, an American named Charles Goodyear accidentally dropped a mixture of rubber and sulfur onto a hot stove. That produced the first bit of vulcanized rubber, a tough material that barely changes with the weather.

Companies still collect latex (left). They make it into natural-rubber products. Most rubber today is synthetic, however. Rubber goes into thousands of products, including a wide assortment of erasers (below).

85

SAFETY PIN

The trouble with the first safety pins was that they weren't safe. The sharp tips poked out. They sometimes scratched or pricked the skin. People in Europe used such pins nearly 4,000 years ago.

In 1849, a New Yorker named Walter Hunt designed a pin with a clasp to enclose the point. Hunt might not have come up with the idea if he hadn't owed money. His creditor—the man from whom he had borrowed $15—made an offer. He'd cancel the debt and pay $400 for all rights to any useful device into which Hunt could shape an old piece of wire. After three hours of twisting, Hunt devised the modern safety pin. He collected the $400. His creditor, it seems, made a fortune.

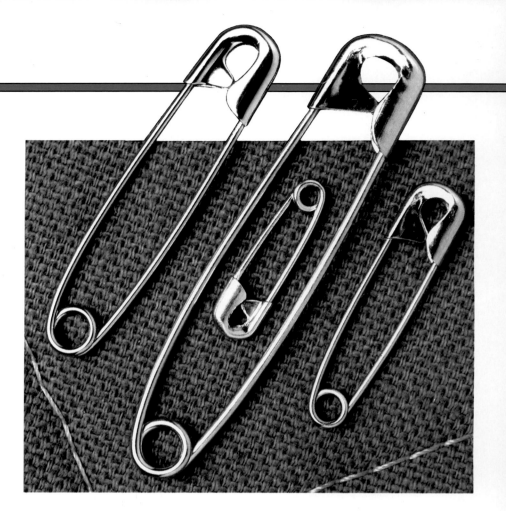

SOAP

A scrub-down with ashes and boiled animal fat may not sound like an especially pleasant way to bathe. Yet these were the chief ingredients of the first soaps. The story of soap goes back a long way: **1.** People in parts of the Middle East probably used an ashes-and-fat cleansing substance 5,000 years ago. **2.** A gritty, soaplike paste helped ancient Egyptians keep clean and treat skin disease. **3.** According to a Roman legend, people sometimes gathered on a mountaintop to sacrifice animals to their gods. Rain washed animal fat and ashes into a river below. Some of the mixture settled on the riverbank. Women used the mixture to launder clothes. **4.** In Europe in the Middle Ages, soapmaking became a craft. Varieties of soaps appeared for bathing, laundering, and shaving. **5.** In England in the 1600s, people had to pay heavy taxes on soap. It was considered a luxury item. **6.** Soapmakers arrived at the new American colony in Jamestown, Virginia, in the early 1600s. But for many years, most Americans made their own soap at home. **7.** In 1791, French chemist Nicolas Leblanc patented a process for using common salt in the making of soap. Soapmaking became easier and less expensive. The process brought the price of soap way down. Nearly everyone could keep clean cheaply.

SANDWICH

He was a devoted gambler, the Fourth Earl of Sandwich. In fact, this English nobleman liked gambling so much that he wouldn't stop for meals. One day, while deeply involved in a card game, he ordered a servant to bring him meat and two pieces of bread. He slapped the meat between the bread slices. *Presto!*—the Earl had a meal he could hold in one hand, leaving the other hand free to play cards.

That happened about 200 years ago. People had probably been eating sandwiches long before then. But it was the Earl who gave the creation its name and made the sandwich popular for busy people everywhere.

The Earl might be surprised to see the great variety of sandwiches people enjoy today. There are hundreds of kinds. Restaurants the world over serve sandwiches. Some sandwiches have funny names: sloppy joe, poor boy, bender schmender, tempting twosome. There are tiny finger sandwiches, and giant heroes—also called submarines or hoagies—that may feed 25 people.

The world's champion sandwich maker is probably Dagwood Bumstead (above). This cartoon character throws in just about everything from the refrigerator to build a masterpiece. The result: a meal that is a true monument to the Fourth Earl of Sandwich.

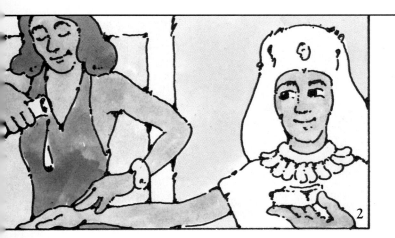

TELEVISION

Standing at the blackboard in his classroom, Philo Farnsworth amazed his teacher. The 16-year-old Idaho farm boy was sketching the details of a television camera. The amazing thing was that television did not yet exist! Farnsworth had formed his idea after reading an article about electron tubes written by a Russian professor. Farnsworth kept working on his idea. In 1930, at age 24, he patented his electronic television camera.

The professor, Boris Rosing, influenced someone else, too. It was one of his students, Vladimir Zworykin. In 1919, Zworykin came to the United States. He began his own experiments. At about the same time as Farnsworth, Zworykin came up with his own camera. Each invention had certain features the other did not have.

Farnsworth and Zworykin pioneered electronic TV. Actually, the idea of television was not new. Work on transmitting images began around 1884. However, no system proved practical until Farnsworth and Zworykin entered the scene.

TV brings us news and entertainment. In the first sets (right), the screen was usually small, and the parts were big. Many modern sets (above) are small and lightweight. You can take them almost anywhere.

TYPEWRITER

In Milwaukee, in 1867, C. Latham Sholes read a magazine article about a machine for printing letters. Inspired by the article, Sholes set out to build a writing machine himself. He made the first one for experimental purposes. It printed only the letter W. In 1868, Sholes, working with two other men, patented a machine that had 11 keys (top). It typed only in capitals, and the typist couldn't see what had been typed without lifting the carriage.

Over the next five years, Sholes built dozens of typewriters. Each was better than the one before. When he finally produced a practical model, a manufacturer bought patent rights to it. Once the typewriter caught on, it changed the business world forever. No longer did letters have to be copied slowly and expensively by hand.

Typewriters in use today range from old-fashioned manuals (above) to computerized electronic word processors (above, right). Whichever typewriter is your type, you'll find that most have one thing in common: the arrangement of letters. Sholes invented an arrangement that helped prevent the keys from banging into each other. It also put frequently used letters within easy reach. Sholes came up with something else that's still around. It's the name he gave his machine: Type-Writer.

TRAFFIC LIGHT

The traffic light is a bright idea for preventing accidents, but it didn't seem so at the start. One of the first traffic signals had mechanical arms for daytime and a gaslight for nighttime. It was installed in London, England, in 1868. It soon blew up, killing a policeman.

The first electric traffic light went up in Cleveland, Ohio, in 1914. It had two lights: red and green. Policemen had to work early lights by hand (far left). By 1926, automatic signals, which did not need an operator, were flashing on busy streets in the United States and Europe.

Today's traffic lights (left) can do more than just shine red, yellow, and green at fixed intervals. Some have devices that give the green light to an approaching emergency vehicle. Many lights change according to traffic conditions to help speed traffic flow. In some cities, a central office controls signal changes by computer.

We think of traffic lights as directing cars, trucks, and buses. But the first lights directed horse-drawn vehicles. Traffic lights in Venice, Italy, direct canal boats.

THERMOMETER

Have a fever? Is it freezing outside? A thermometer will give you a quick, accurate answer. In the mid-1600s, an Italian nobleman, Ferdinand II, hit on the idea of sealing liquid in a glass tube to measure temperature. Ferdinand's device contained water and alcohol. Today, most thermometers contain mercury.

At first, scientists disagreed on what they should use as a basis for measurement. Should it be the melting point of butter? Perhaps blood temperature? Or the temperature of fixed points of the Paris Observatory? Finally, scientists agreed to base measurement on the freezing and the boiling points of water at sea level. That resulted in the scale used on most thermometers today.

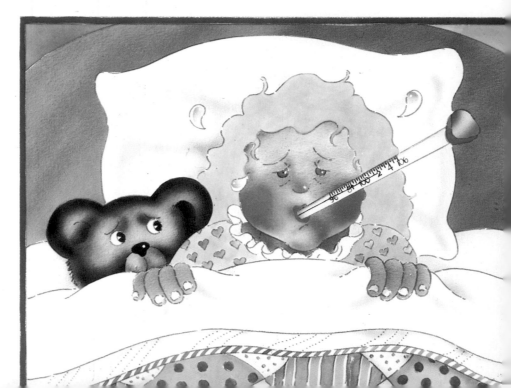

U UNDERWATER PHOTOGRAPHY

"Say 'fish.'" Loaded down with diving gear and waterproof cameras and lights, a photographer makes a picture on the ocean floor (below). The result is a close-up of a shrimp and a fish called a goby (right).

Around the turn of the century, French scientist Louis Boutan made a big splash with the invention of equipment for underwater photography. Boutan wanted to photograph scenes never before witnessed. No one had made pictures deep underwater before, and that gave Boutan his challenge. It took him almost eight years to perfect, but by 1899 Boutan had what he wanted: a watertight box for a camera, as well as lights for underwater photography. Boutan's inventions opened up a whole new world for photographers. More important, they led to improved equipment that helps scientists probe secrets of the mysterious sea.

UMBRELLA

Come rain or shine, people pop open umbrellas. Americans use umbrellas mostly to protect themselves from rain (right). In some warm regions, people use umbrellas as protection from the sun, as well.

Umbrellas were first used thousands of years ago, perhaps in China. In some countries, the style and color of an umbrella showed wealth and rank. A ruler might have an especially fancy umbrella, decorated with jewels and embroidery.

In the late 1700s, umbrellas became fashionable in England. At first, the umbrella had many foes. Drivers of horse-drawn cabs feared that the product would take away their business. If people could stay dry on foot, why would they hire a cab? The drivers needn't have worried. If you visit London today, you'll find taxicabs—and umbrellas—aplenty.

V

VACUUM CLEANER

If you had tried out a vacuum cleaner of the 1800s, it probably would have tried your patience. Those early machines worked by hand or foot power. They often spread more dust than they collected. In 1901, an Englishman named Hubert Booth patented an electrically powered machine that sucked in dust and filtered it. But his machine was so big that it had to be pulled from building to building by horses.

Credit a janitor named James Murray Spangler for developing a vacuum cleaner small enough for home use. Spangler suffered from coughing spells. For years, he had used a carpet sweeper to clean the floors of a store in Canton, Ohio. Breathing dust kicked up by the sweeper made the bad cough worse. Seeking a dustless way to clean, he built a vacuum cleaner from a fan motor, a soap box, a broom handle, and a pillowcase. The machine did the job. Spangler patented his invention in 1908. He went into business with William Hoover, who had bought manufacturing rights. The Hoover machine (right), and other models, caught on. Ever since, they've been making a clean sweep as household necessities.

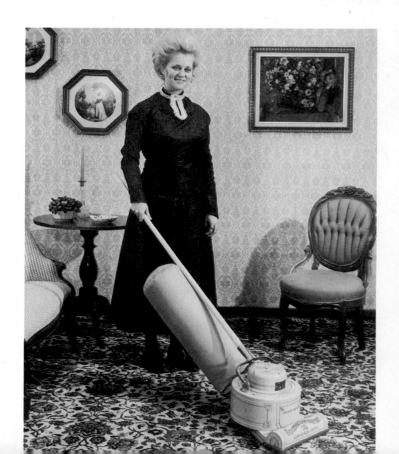

VACCINATION

Eight-year-old James Phipps winces as he receives the first smallpox vaccination. The year is 1796. Doctor Edward Jenner, of Berkeley, England, conducts the experiment.

Smallpox had been a dreaded disease for centuries. Many victims, mostly children, died. Survivors were scarred for life and sometimes blinded. Early treatments called for putting pus from an infected person onto the skin of a healthy person. The healthy person was supposed to develop immunity to the disease. With immunity, a person's body resists infection. But the treatment itself was sometimes deadly.

Jenner had heard milkmaids claim they would never catch smallpox since they had already had cowpox. That is a milder, related infection. After studying their claims, Jenner vaccinated Phipps. He put pus from the hand of a cowpox-infected milkmaid into scratches on Phipps's arm. It worked! The boy became immune to smallpox.

Thanks to Jenner's discovery and to international vaccination efforts, the world in 1980 was officially declared free of smallpox.

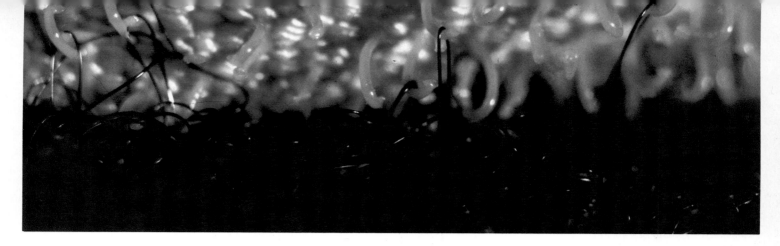

VELCRO FASTENER

In 1948, a Swiss engineer, George de Mestral, took a hunting trip in the Alps. As he made his way over the mountains, seedpods called burrs stuck to his clothes. De Mestral wondered why. A close look showed tiny hooks on each burr clinging to thread loops in his clothing. The burrs gave de Mestral a ripping good idea. He set out to invent a fastener that would work like a burr. After about eight years, he developed Velcro (a registered trademark). A tape with many hooks sticks to one with many loops (above). The tapes separate with a *rrrrrip!* They can be used over and over. Manufacturers use Velcro fasteners in jackets (left), in shoes, in space suits, even in artificial hearts.

W

WINDSHIELD WIPER

On a rainy-day ride in an early automobile, the driver had to squint through streaked glass. The passenger risked a fall while wiping the glass by hand (right, top). Mary Anderson, of Birmingham, Alabama, tried to make soggy rides safer. In 1903, she invented one of the first windshield wipers. But it was hand operated and inconvenient. In 1917, a Hawaiian dentist invented an electric wiper (right, bottom). Apparently, he never marketed it. An inventor patented a wiper with a vacuum-operated motor in the 1920s. The vacuum wiper became standard equipment on many models. Then someone took another look at the electric wiper. A company began making electric wipers in 1924. Today, most windshield wipers are electrically powered.

94

WHEEL

Thinking of a world without wheels is enough to make your head spin. Other basic inventions—the knife, for example—appeared earlier, but none has been so useful in so many ways. Before the wheel, people had to carry loads on their backs or drag them on sleds. With the wheel, they could use carts to move much heavier loads. Today, nearly every piece of machinery requires wheels in some form for its operation.

The wheel first appeared more than 5,000 years ago in the Middle East. Early wheels used for transport were made of pieces of wood clamped together to form a circle (below). People soon added shaped wooden rims to make the wheels wear evenly. Then people found new uses for the wheel. In the Middle East, it was used as a potter's wheel. Other devices followed, such as the windmill and the pulley.

Inflatable automobile tires (left) first came along in the late 1800s. Compare this tire with the ancient wooden wheel. The basic design has remained unchanged since the wheel's beginnings in the distant past.

Your Washing Done for 2c a Week by the Wonderful 1900 Electric Motor Washer

Free Book Tells All About it

Just a "Twist of the Wrist" Starts or Stops the Machine
—That's All the Work You Do.   And the Motor Runs the Wringer, too!

The 1900 Electric Motor Washer is now at work in thousands of homes. It is doing the work formerly done by well-paid washerwomen, **at a cost of 2 cents a week for electricity.** Saving thousands upon thousands of dollars in wash bills. Saving worlds of wash-day troubles.

WASHING MACHINE

Not too long ago, people didn't feel wishy-washy about washday—they clearly hated it. They had to lug water in buckets, heat it, and rub clothes against a washboard (left, top). It was backbreaking work. Many American inventors tried to find ways to ease the burden. By 1873, some 2,000 patents had been issued for washing machines. Most of these machines were clumsy devices with washer blades that had to be turned by hand. In the early 1900s, electric machines began to lighten the washday work load. Advertisements (above) proclaimed the wonders of these machines. But it was not until about 1937 that manufacturers came up with fully automatic washing machines. Within a few years, the old washboard was washed up for good. Washing machines today (left, bottom) wash and rinse clothes automatically. Some machines also dry them. Many machines can be programmed to treat fabrics with tender, loving care.

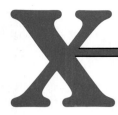

XEROGRAPHIC COPIER

Paperwork, paperwork, paperwork! That's what Chester Carlson's office was all about. Carlson worked at a patent office in New York City. He noticed that employees often needed extra copies of patent applications. Copying methods then in use were slow and messy. Carlson believed he could improve on them. He hoped to invent a quick, dry copying process that would combine electricity and principles of photography. In 1935, he set up a lab in his kitchen.

Three years later, Carlson produced his first photocopy with a crude machine he had designed. Though blurry, the copy proved to him that his technique worked. With the help of a research institute, Carlson improved his process.

The process was named "xerography" (zih-RAHG-ruh-fee), from the Greek words for "dry writing." Even with the improvements, the process was not yet ready for the marketplace. In 1947, a small manufacturing company joined in the effort to develop the copier. More years passed. Finally, in 1959, the manufacturers produced the first fully automatic office copying machine.

With xerographic copiers, people can make instant copies of anything from newsletters (below) to photographs. Some machines can reduce or enlarge an original to the desired size. Some copiers print in color—and some even sort page copies and arrange them into booklets.

Y

YO–YO

You might say that, as an object for fun, the yo-yo has had its ups and downs. Today, it's a popular toy. But the yo-yo may have started out as a deadly weapon. It is believed that people in the Philippine Islands used the yo-yo thousands of years ago for hunting and for fighting. They made a yo-yo out of chipped rock and a long leather cord. A hunter or a warrior in a tree used the yo-yo to strike prey or an enemy below. If the thrower's aim were off, he could at least pull the weapon back easily. Over time, use of the yo-yo as a weapon declined. Some people still used it to settle disputes—but in tournaments of skill rather than in warfare. Eventually, the yo-yo came to be used as a toy only.

Children in ancient Greece played with yo-yos. So, perhaps, did children in ancient China. In California, in the late 1920s, a businessman named Donald Duncan watched a Filipino demonstrate tricks with a yo-yo. Duncan guessed that the yo-yo would be a hit with Americans, and he began to manufacture it. He guessed right. The yo-yo's popularity went spinning to new heights. Since 1929, the company Duncan started has sold more than half a *billion* yo-yos!

Z

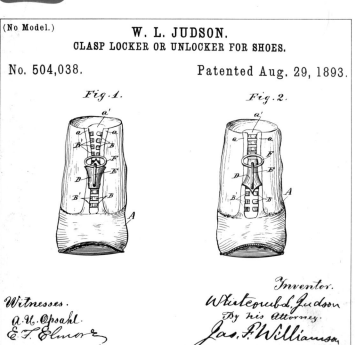

(No Model.)

W. L. JUDSON.
CLASP LOCKER OR UNLOCKER FOR SHOES.

No. 504,038.   Patented Aug. 29, 1893.

Fig.1.   *Fig.2.*

Witnesses.
A. U. Opsahl.
E. F. Elmore

Inventor.
Whitcomb L. Judson
By his Attorney.
Jas. F. Williamson

ZIPPER

Too awkward! Too time-consuming! That's what Whitcomb Judson thought was wrong with the series of laces, hooks, and eyes with which people of the 1800s fastened their clothes. Judson, a Chicago inventor, set about to work on the problem. The result: an 1893 patent for a "clasp locker or unlocker for shoes"—the first zipper (left). Trouble was, it often came undone unexpectedly. People wouldn't buy it, and Judson nearly went broke. Swedish engineer Gideon Sundback came to the rescue. In 1913, he patented a fastener almost identical to today's zippers (right). The Navy tested an improved version for flying suits—and bought it. The B. F. Goodrich Company used it in rubber boots. Also, someone in the company gave the fastener a new name: zipper. From then on, the device had no trouble buttoning up a large share of the fastener market.

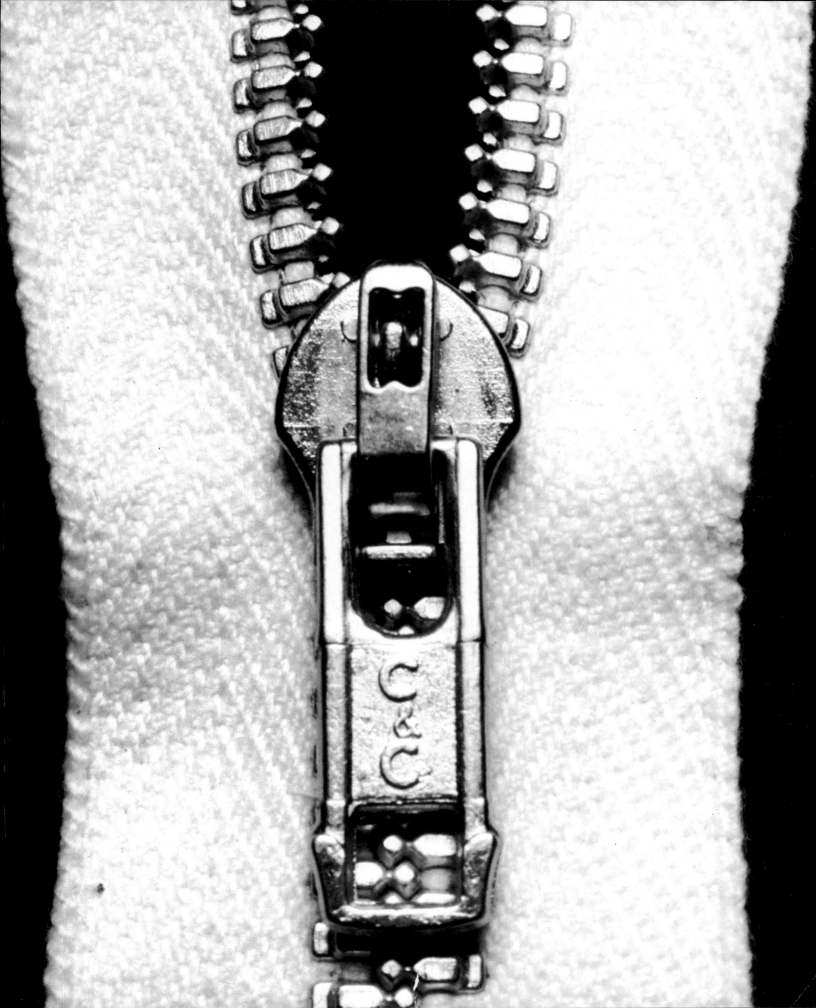

ILLUSTRATIONS CREDITS

CONTENTS PAGE

Manfred Kage/Peter Arnold, Inc. (2–3).

THE INVENTORS

Library of Congress (6, 26 top); Culver Pictures (7 left and low right); Chris Collins/The Stock Market (7 top right); Courtesy Smithsonian Institution, No. 77-7737 (7 center right); James A. Sugar/Black Star (13 low); Charles E. Herron, National Geographic Staff (14–15, 15 right, both); Courtesy Pontiac Motor Division, General Motors Corporation (20–21, except 20 low left); Courtesy Sarah Callahan/Patent Reproduction Company (28–29 all).

THE STORY OF PLASTICS

Society of the Plastics Industry, Inc. (33 center right); Ed Bohon/The Stock Market (36 left); Harold Roth/Black Star (36–37); Courtesy Borg-Warner (37 top right); Marmel Studios/FPG Int'l (37 low right); Albert Moldvay (38); Ted Horowitz/The Stock Market (43 low right); Brad Hess/Black Star (45).

INVENTIONS FROM A TO Z

Sharon Davis, art (48–49, 78, 94); National Geographic Photographer James L. Amos (49 top, 64 top right); Jonathan Blair (50 top); Elyse Lewin/The Image Bank (51 top left); Courtesy Smithsonian Institution, No. 75-15620 (51 right); Daniel Productions (51 low); Georges Tourdjman/The Image Bank (52 left); Sue Levin, art (53, 54, 67, 72, 97); Wendell Metzen/Southern Stock Photos (54 top right); Leo Touchet/Photo-Corp Services, Inc. (54 center); George O'Bremski/The Image Bank (55).

James A. Sugar/Black Star (56 top, 61 all, 65 top, 67 left, 70 right, 72 top, 74 right, 80 top, 82 top); Gary Gladstone/The Image Bank (56 low left, 84 top left); Michael Melford/The Image Bank (56 low right); Jim Tuten/Southern Stock Photos (57 all); Courtesy Smithsonian Institution, No. 75-3665 (58 top left).

John Launois/Black Star (58 top right); Gloria Marconi, art (58 low, 81, 90); Dane A. Penland (59); Stockphotos/Jerry Wolfe (60 left); Kasz Maciag/The Stock Market (60 right); Ken Clark (62); Barbara Gibson, art (63, 64 low, 65 low, 66); J. Sherwood Chalmers (66 top left); Ira Block (68 top); Courtesy Levi Strauss & Co. (68 low); John Earle/The Stock Market (69 top); Arthur d'Arazien/The Image Bank (69 low); Charles E. Herron, National Geographic Staff (70 left); Martin Rogers (71 left).

American Heritage Center of the University of Wyoming/Emmett D. Chisum, Research Historian (71 top right); Charles R. Lee, art (73); Lemere/FPG Int'l (74 left); Tony Linck/Shostal (75); FPG Int'l (76 low); Courtesy Smithsonian Institution, Nos. 79-7875, 79-7859, 79-1974, 79-7848 (77 top all); Don Gates, art (79 low); National Geographic Photographer Bruce Dale (79 top); Tim McCabe/Soil Conservation Service (80 center); Frank Whitney/The Image Bank (80 low).

Stockphotos/Link (81 left); Courtesy American Plywood Association (81 top right); Joseph F. Ochlak, National Geographic Staff, art (82 low left); Andy Levin/Black Star (83 top); National Museum of Roller Skating, Lincoln, Nebraska (83 low left); Michael Yada (83 low right); Mark Romanelli/The Image Bank (84 top right); Stockphotos/Carroll Seghers (84 low); Courtesy The Firestone Tire & Rubber Company (85 left); Bill Burrows, art adapted from "Soaps and Detergents," © 1981, The Soap and Detergent Association (86–87 low); © King Features Syndicate (87 top).

Donal F. Holway (88 left); Fred J. Maroon (88 right); Courtesy Sarah Callahan/Patent Reproduction Company (89 top right, 98 low); Louis Van Camp/Shostal (89 center, both); Courtesy Crouse-Hinds Co. (90 top left); Shmuel Thaler/Pacific Light Views (90 top right); David Doubilet (91 both); Frank T. Wood/Shostal (92 top); Culver Pictures (92 low); © 1960, reprinted Courtesy Parke-Davis Division, Warner-Lambert Company (93); J. Barry O'Rourke/The Stock Market (95 left); Courtesy Trustees of the British Museum (95 right); McClure's 1898–1900 (96 top); Bill Burrows, art (96 left).

ADDITIONAL READING

Readers may want to check the *National Geographic Index* in a school or a public library for related articles and to refer to the following books. ("A" indicates a book for readers at the adult level.)

American Heritage, *Men of Science and Invention*, 1966. Ashley, Clifford W., *The Ashley Book of Knots*, Doubleday, 1944 (A). Asimov, Isaac, *Asimov's Biographical Encyclopedia of Science and Technology*, Doubleday, 1982 (A). Barnouw, Erik, *A History of Broadcasting in the United States*, Oxford University Press, 1966 (vol. 1), 1968 (vol. 2), 1970 (vol. 3) (A). Baxby, Derrick, *Jenner's Smallpox Vaccine: The Riddle of Vaccinia Virus and its Origin*, Heinemann Educational Books, 1981 (A).

Behrman, Carol H., *The Remarkable Writing Machine*, Julian Messner, 1981. Bolsen, Victor, *William P. Lear: From High School Dropout to Space-Age Inventor*, Hawthorn, 1974. Boyd, Thomas A., *Professional Amateur: The Biography of Charles Franklin Kettering*, Ayer, 1972 (A). Boyne, Walter J., and Donald S. Lopez, eds., *The Jet Age: Forty Years of Jet Aviation*, National Air and Space Museum, Smithsonian Institution Press, 1979 (A). Bradbury, S., *The Microscope Past and Present*, Pergamon Press, 1969 (A).

Bramson, Ann, *Soap*, Workman, 1975 (A). Brown, A. F. Anderson, *The Incubation Book*, State Mutual Book & Periodical Service, 1981 (A). Cipolla, Carlo M., and Derek Birdsall, *The Technology of Man: A Visual History*, Holt, Rinehart and Winston, 1980 (A). Clabby, John, *The Natural History of the Horse*, Taplinger, 1976 (A). Clarke, Donald, ed., *The Encyclopedia of How It Works: From Abacus to Zoom Lens*, A&W, 1977. Cook, David, *Inventions That Made History*, Putnam, 1968. Cousins, Margaret, *The Story of Thomas Alva Edison*, Random House, 1981.

Cox, James A., *A Century of Light*, Benjamin, 1979 (A). Dahnsen, Alan, *Bicycles*, Franklin Watts, 1978. De Bono, Edward, *Eureka! An Illustrated History of Inventions from the Wheel to the Computer*, Holt, Rinehart and Winston, 1974 (A). Doster, Alexis III, Joe Goodwin, and Jane M. Ross, eds., *Smithsonian Book of Invention*, W. W. Norton, 1978 (A). Ellis, Keith, *Thomas Edison, Genius of Electricity*, Priory Press, 1974. Englebardt, Stanley L., *Miracle Chip: The Microelectronic Revolution*, Lothrop, Lee & Shepard, 1979 (A). Feldman, Anthony, and Peter Eord, *Scientists and Inventors*, Facts on File, 1979 (A). Ford, Barbara, *The Elevator*, Walker, 1982.

Frandos, Joel, *The Story of the Plastics Industry*, Society of the Plastics Industry, Inc., 1977 (A). Friedel, Robert, *Pioneer Plastic: The Making and Selling of Celluloid*, University of Wisconsin Press, 1983 (A). Gardner, Robert, *This Is the Way It Works: a Collection of Machines*, Doubleday, 1980. Garrison, Webb, *Why Didn't I Think of That? From Alarm Clocks to Zippers*, Prentice-Hall, 1977. Giedion, Siegfried, *Mechanization Takes Command*, W. W. Norton, 1969 (A). Gleasner, Diana C., *Dynamite*, Walker, 1982. Harrison, Molly, *Home Inventions*, Usborne, 1975. Hecht, Jeff, and Dick Teresi, *Laser: Supertool of the 1980s*, Ticknor and Fields, 1982 (A).

Henry, Joanne Landers, *Robert Fulton: Steamboat Builder*, Garrard, 1975. Hoffman-Axthelm, Walter, *History of Dentistry*, Quintessence, 1981 (A). Hogan, Paula, Z., *The Compass*, Walker, 1982. Holmes, Maynard, and Christopher Edward, *Great Men of Science*, Franklin Watts, 1979. *The Illustrated Science and Invention Encyclopedia: How it Works*, H. S. Stuttman, 1976 (A). Johnson, Spencer, *The Value of Patience: The Story of the Wright Brothers*, Value Communications, 1976 (A). Moskowitz, Milton, et al., eds., *Everybody's Business*, Harper and Row, 1980 (A). Murphy, Jim, *Weird and Wacky Inventions*, Crown, 1978. Norman, Bruce, *The Inventing of America*, Taplinger, 1976 (A).

O'Brien, Robert, *Machines*, Time-Life, 1980 (A). Ott, Virginia, and Gloria Swanson, *Man With a Million Ideas: Fred Jones, Genius/Inventor*, Lerner, 1977 (A). Pick, Christopher C., *Undersea Machines*, Raintree, 1979 (A). Quackenbush, Robert, *Along Came the Model T: How Henry Ford Put the World on Wheels*, Parents, 1978 (A). Starr, Chester G., *A History of the Ancient World*, Oxford University Press, 1974 (A).

Turner, Roland, and Steven L. Goulden, eds., *Great Engineers: From Antiquity Through the Industrial Revolution*, vol. 1, St. Martin's Press, 1981 (A). Weiss, Harvey, *How to Be an Inventor*, Crowell, 1980. Williams, Brian, *Inventions and Discoveries*, Franklin Watts, 1979 (A). Zerwick, Chloe, *A Short History of Glass*, the Corning Museum of Glass, 1980 (A).

NATIONAL GEOGRAPHIC BOOKS

Exploring the Deep Frontier: The Adventure of Man in the Sea, 1980 (A). *How Things are Made*, 1981. *How Things Work*, 1983. *Nature's Healing Arts: From Folk Medicine to Modern Drugs*, 1977 (A). *On the Brink of Tomorrow: Frontiers of Science*, 1982 (A). *Peoples and Places of the Past*, 1983 (A). *Those Inventive Americans*, 1971 (A).

Library of Congress CIP Data

Main entry under title:

Small inventions that make a big difference.

  (Books for world explorers)

  Bibliography: p.

  Includes index.

  SUMMARY: Describes how inventors think and work, explains how one invention—plastic—has changed the world, and briefly discusses seventy-five other important inventions, from the jet engine to the potato chip.

  1. Inventions—Juvenile literature. 2. Inventors—Juvenile literature. [1. Inventions. 2. Inventors. 3. Plastics] I. Bailey, Joseph H., ill.

II. Huehnergarth, John, ill. III. National Geographic Society (U. S.) IV. Series.

T212.S63 1984   608   83–23770

ISBN 0-87044-498-0 (regular edition)

ISBN 0-87044-503-0 (library edition)

Composition for SMALL INVENTIONS THAT MAKE A BIG DIFFERENCE by National Geographic's Photographic Services, Carl M. Shrader, Director; Lawrence F. Ludwig, Assistant Director. Printed and bound by Holladay-Tyler Printing Corp., Rockville, Md. Color separations by the Lanman-Progressive Co., Washington, D. C.; Lincoln Graphics, Inc., Cherry Hill, N.J.; and NEC, Inc., Nashville, Tenn. FAR-OUT FUN! printed by McCollum Press, Inc., Rockville, Md.; Classroom Activities folder produced by Mazer Corp., Dayton, Ohio.

INDEX

CONSULTANTS

Thomas V. DiBacco, American University—*Chief Consultant*

Glenn O. Blough, LL.D., University of Maryland; Phyllis G. Sidorsky, National Cathedral School; Violet A. Tibbetts—*Educational Consultants*

Nicholas J. Long, Ph.D.—*Consulting Psychologist*

The Special Publications and School Services Division is grateful to the individuals named or quoted within the text and to those cited here for their generous assistance:

Thomas Abbott, Xerox Corporation; Mary C. Ansbro, Soap and Detergent Association; Pat Bowlin, American Plywood Association; Doris Bowman, Smithsonian Institution; Robert H. Brill, Corning Museum of Glass; Michael W. Brooslin, National Museum of Roller Skating; Fran Cannon, Braille Institute; Charles Chandler, American Lock Collectors Association; Scott Chou, Seiko Time Corporation; Thomas Clarke, General Motors Corporation; John Conkling, American Pyrotechnics Association; William Cooke, International Museum of the Horse, Kentucky Horse Park; Frank Corbin, Society of the Plastics Industry, Inc.; Diane M. Dickey, Kellogg Company.

C. W. "Smokey" Doyle, Fort Worth, Texas; James C. Elliott, Goddard Space Flight Center; Bernard S. Finn, Smithsonian Institution; Michael Fitzmaurice, Goddard Space Flight Center; Cecil Fox, Armed Forces Institute of Pathology; Robert Friedel, Institute of Electrical and Electronics Engineers; Anthony V. Gagliardi, General Motors Technical Center.

John F. Graham, Society of the Plastics Industry, Inc.; Ray Gummer, Duncan Toys Company; Albert O. Halstead, Crouse-Hinds Company; Raymond J. Hebert, Smithsonian Institution; David Holloway, University of Maryland; Kathleen A. Horning, E. I. du Pont de Nemours & Company; Richard Howell, Farm and Industrial Equipment Institute; Paul L. Kelley, Aluminum Association, Inc.; Terry G. Kelley, Sterling Drug, Inc.; Jack Keville, Plastic Museum; Michael K. Kirk, U. S. Patent and Trademark Office; Judy Klein, General Foods Corporation; William J. Knight, General Motors Technical Center; Ramunas A. Kondratas, Smithsonian Institution; Robert Kramer, NCR Corporation; Stacy Krammes, Hoover Historical Center; Thomas Kraner, American Paper Institute.

Joan Lambert, Outdoor Power Equipment Institute, Inc.; Keith Lauer, Leominster, Mass.; Bruce MacDonald, Pontiac Motor Division, General Motors Corporation; William S. MacNaughton, Levi Strauss & Co.; Lois Mann, AC&R Public Relations, Inc.; Luis Marden, National Geographic Society; Oscar Mastin, U. S. Patent and Trademark Office; Edwin L. Moore, State of Florida Department of Citrus; James Morrand, University of Cincinnati; Stan Nelson, Smithsonian Institution; Barbara Anne Neuwald, Evinrude; W. Frederick Oettele, E. I. du Pont de Nemours & Company; Eugene Ostroff, Smithsonian Institution; Doyle Peck, Braille Institute; Dom Pisano, Smithsonian Institution.

Boyd Ringo, University of Cincinnati; Denise Schmandt-Besserat, University of Texas at Austin; G. L. Scott, Velcro USA, Inc.; Dean Shupe, University of Cincinnati; Elliot Sivowitch, Smithsonian Institution; Jenifer Stermer, International Museum of the Horse, Kentucky Horse Park; George E. Stuart, National Geographic Society; Louis Takacs, E. I. du Pont de Nemours & Company; Dick Thompson, Pontiac Motor Division, General Motors Corporation; Peter Thompson, Otis Elevator Company; Lois M. Vann, Smithsonian Institution; Gaylon H. White, Goodyear Tire & Rubber Company; Lois M. White, National Hearing Aid Society; Roger White, Smithsonian Institution; Ilene Zeldin, Battelle Memorial Institute.

SMALL INVENTIONS THAT MAKE A BIG DIFFERENCE

PUBLISHED BY
THE NATIONAL GEOGRAPHIC SOCIETY
WASHINGTON, D. C.

Gilbert M. Grosvenor, *President*
Melvin M. Payne, *Chairman of the Board*
Owen R. Anderson, *Executive Vice President*
Robert L. Breeden, *Vice President,
Publications and Educational Media*

PREPARED BY THE SPECIAL PUBLICATIONS
AND SCHOOL SERVICES DIVISION

Donald J. Crump, *Director*
Philip B. Silcott, *Associate Director*
William L. Allen, William R. Gray, *Assistant Directors*

STAFF FOR BOOKS FOR WORLD EXPLORERS
Ralph Gray, *Editor*
Pat Robbins, *Managing Editor*
Ursula Perrin Vosseler, *Art Director*

STAFF FOR *SMALL INVENTIONS THAT MAKE A BIG DIFFERENCE*
Ross Bankson, *Managing Editor*
Charles E. Herron, *Picture Editor*
Mary Elizabeth Molloy, *Designer*
Mary Lee Elden, Tee Loftin, *Researchers*
Joan Hurst, *Editorial Assistant*
Artemis S. Lampathakis, *Illustrations Assistant*
Janet A. Dustin, *Art Secretary*
Carole J. King, *Intern*

STAFF FOR *FAR-OUT FUN!* Patricia N. Holland, *Project Editor;* Jane R. McGoldrick, *Text Editor;* Mary Elizabeth Molloy, *Designer;* Dru Colbert, *Artist*

ENGRAVING, PRINTING, AND PRODUCT MANUFACTURE
Robert W. Messer, *Manager;* George V. White, *Production Manager;* Mary A. Bennett, *Production Project Manager;* Mark R. Dunlevy, David V. Showers, Gregory Storer, George J. Zeller, Jr., *Assistant Production Managers;* Julia F. Warner, *Production Staff Assistant*

STAFF ASSISTANTS: Nancy F. Berry, Pamela A. Black, Mary Frances Brennan, Lori E. Davie, Mary Elizabeth Davis, Rosamund Garner, Victoria D. Garrett, Nancy J. Harvey, Sandra K. Huhn, Katherine R. Leitch, Virginia W. McCoy, Mary Evelyn McKinney, Cleo Petroff, Sheryl A. Prohovich, Carol Rocheleau Curtis, Kathleen T. Shea, Linda L. Whittington

MARKET RESEARCH: Mark W. Brown, Joseph S. Fowler, Carrla L. Holmes, Meg McElligott Kieffer, Nancy Serbin, Susan D. Snell, Barbara Steinwurtzel

INDEX: Charles M. Israel, Jr.